MOSQUITO POINT ROAD

Monroe County Murder & Mayhem

Michael Benson

A portion of this book previously appeared in
(585) Magazine.

Cover design by Tekla Benson
Cover photo by Christine Green

Benson Book #2001

ISBN: 979-8-6302-9811-9

Printed in the U.S.A.

Table of Contents

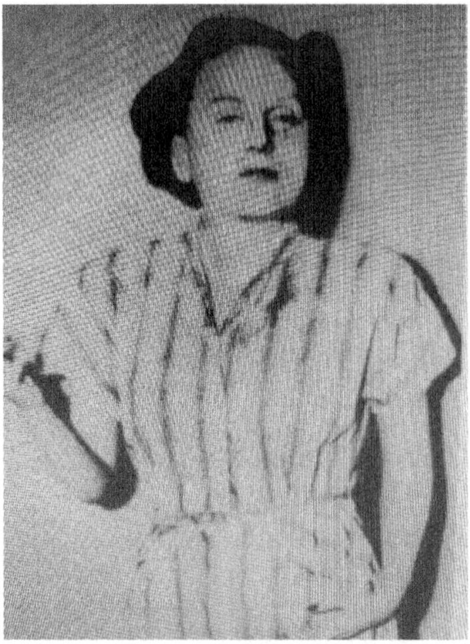

Jean Hetenyi

KILLER OF THE CLOTH

I first heard of the murder of Jean Hetenyi during the summer of 1962 when I was five years old and walking with my mother down Stallman Drive, the dirt road on which we lived in rural Chili, N.Y. My father, an adjuster for the Insurance Company of North America, had moved us only weeks before from Campbell Street in the Dutchtown section of Rochester out to the country. He bought a house and four acres off of Ballantyne Road.

The north edge of our property was bordered by Black Creek as it flowed past Genesee Junction to the river a half mile to the east. Our street was L-shaped with only four houses on it. The mailboxes were up on Ballantyne Road, so there was a walk involved in getting the mail every afternoon, and that's where my mom and I were headed.

On the outside of Stallman Drive's bend was a run-down house that had no indoor plumbing. There was a water pump in the back and an outhouse. During the long, cold Chili winters, a pot-bellied stove was all they had for heat. This was where the Tylers lived, Ol' Lady Tyler and her two youngest children, who were teenagers at the time.

Ol' Lady Tyler was mentally ill. She once asked my mother if she could come into our house and allow her to listen for Martians in our washing machine. As my mother and I walked down the road Ol' Lady Tyler was out front and waved for us to come talk to her.

"You remember that preacher years ago who was supposed to have killed his wife?" Ol' Lady Tyler asked my mom.

My mom did remember. It had been big news. She remembered it happened when she was seventeen years old, attending Our Lady of Mercy High School and working at Neisner's, a five-and-dime department store on East Main Street in downtown Rochester.

"Sure," my mom said.

"Well, the wife's body was dumped right back there," Ol' Lady Tyler said, pointing an arthritic forefinger toward the creek behind our house.

"Really," my mom said. The lady was nuts. Didn't mean she was wrong.

"I know the preacher didn't kill that woman, you know why?"

My mom shook her head nervously.

"Because I know who did," Ol' Lady Tyler said, and then added a witchy cackle.

With that I felt my mom's hand tighten on mine and we started walking again toward the mailboxes.

"I get it," Mrs. Tyler said. "Little pitchers have big ears."

I wondered how Mrs. Tyler knew I was a pitcher – well, I wanted to be one anyway.

I later learned that Ol' Lady Tyler was "obsessed" with the murder of Jean Hetenyi, and had written letters regarding her theories to both neighbors and the sheriff.

One neighbor remembered a deputy coming around asking about Mrs. Tyler. Was there any chance she really knew the things she claimed to know? The vote was unanimous. She was crazy, so her letters were ignored. Unfortunately, nobody remembered what her theories were.

Now, as some of you might know, the Formicolas occupied one of the houses on Stallman Drive and George-Ann Formicola was my babysitter. She and her friend Kathy Bernhard were murdered brutally with a knife. One of the places where the girls were last seen was by the creek behind our house in 1966. I did extensive research on the area in which I grew up when writing The Devil at Genesee Junction, *about those murders.*

I learned how much the area changed after 1952 when the Mt. Morris dam opened and at least some of the plains around Ballantyne Road (formerly known as Mosquito Point Road, name changed in 1926) no longer flooded over every spring.

The land in many spots only became inhabitable after the dam was built. I found that the wilderness behind my childhood home was a hotbed for violent crime:

One guy shot another by the railroad tracks near the ancient stone trestle that crossed the creek just east of my dad's property.

A third wheel in a truly ugly love triangle was found stashed under that trestle in a separate murder.

And during my research I once again came across the extremely odd story of the preacher who did or didn't kill his wife, and did or didn't dump his wife's body in Black Creek seventeen years before Kathy and George-Ann took their last swim back there.

I renewed my interest during the spring of 2020. Stuck inside because of the corona virus pandemic, I exhaustively researched the case.

And this is what I learned…

The Rev. George Paul Hetenyi

It was 9:30 a.m. on Saturday, April 23, 1949. There were a few fluffy clouds in the sky. The air was spring fresh, and the temperature near perfect, in the high sixties. Ten-year-old Leslie L. McMahon was wearing an Eisenhower jacket over a white tee shirt, dungarees, and sneaks. He was carrying a fishing pole and was poking along the West Brighton side of the Genesee River 350 feet from his home at 55 Delaware Avenue, looking for a good place to drop his line. It was a little bit of a trick because the water was so high from the spring melt. The water looked cold, a murky gray, not very clean, but the current was strong. The color darkened on the other side of the river from the inflow of silt from the appropriately named Black Creek. By August, Leslie knew, he'd be able to sit and fish from perches that were still underwater.

He looked to his south where there loomed a black-iron trestle across the river, over which the West Shore railroad chugged its way to and from Genesee Junction. He'd seen bigger kids jump off that bridge. Then he saw something in the river that caught his eye, about twenty feet south of

Delaware Avenue.

"I thought it was a dressmaker's dummy," he remembered seventy-one years later. "Being a kid, I didn't think too much about it."

By his recollection, he was alone, and it didn't occur to him that the "dummy" might be a real person. Not far from the dummy, Les fished for about an hour, didn't catch anything, packed up and headed home. On his way back to the road, he encountered a neighbor lady, Mrs. Clara Beach, who was herself walking along the shoulder of East River Road, having a nice Saturday morning stroll.

"Good morning, Mrs. Beach," Les said. "There's something funny in the water down there."

When Les got home he found his dad getting in the car to go shopping and asked to come along. The McMahons went to the A&P grocery store on South Avenue, and Les was allowed to pick out an airplane model to take home and assemble.

According to his memory, he didn't tell his dad about the thing in the river until they were almost home and saw the sheriff's vehicles along the river. It was then that Les put it together.

"Gosh, Dad, I saw something down there when I was fishing."

They stopped and Les learned that, as he already suspected, the thing he'd seen was not a dummy. He told a deputy—and later a reporter—his story about seeing the body earlier that morning but not realizing what it was.

Leslie McMahon was named in the paper as first to see the body, and later had to testify in court about his "discovery." Three other neighbor kids however, have claimed over the years to have been there when the body was discovered.

Bob Flesch, who was then a thirteen-year-old neighbor of Leslie's, says that he was fishing with Les when they saw the body. Les insists he was alone, although he knew and sometimes hung out with Bob. Bob says his name didn't get in the paper because he was so upset by what he'd seen that he went to his home on Bronx Drive and didn't say anything. He remembered it vividly, the way the body's dress had gotten caught on tree branches that had fallen and clustered in the river.

The third witness is Linda Powell, a girl that both Bob and Les remember, who lived on Delaware Avenue in the house closest to East River Road. Her story is a little different, and may be various memories combined into one. She says there was a baseball game being played on and someone hit the ball very far and it bounced across East River Road. When the kids went to look for the ball, they found the body.

Memories after seventy-one years can be suspect. But is there a way for everyone to be telling the truth. Sure! They all saw the body, that much is for sure. The key, I believe, is that neither Les nor Bob immediately told a parent what they'd seen. Les told Mrs. Beach but not his father, until later.

If Mrs. Beach was the first to call the sheriff, there was time for other kids in the neighborhood to see the body before authorities arrived. Linda could have seen the body from her house. A fourth kid from the neighborhood, Bob Munnings, also laid claim to the discovery, but passed away in 1980.

For the purposes of this story we will go with Les's version. He was the one given credit in the newspaper for discovering the body, and he was the only child who would eventually be called upon to testify in court as to what he'd seen.

I know, it's about as clear as the Genesee River was that spring morning. Getting back to Mrs. Clara Beach, who was having a Saturday morning stroll, and had been the first person Les saw after seeing the thing in the water.

Mrs. Beach had no idea what Les meant by "something funny" and decided to wander over there and see what he was talking about. On her way to the riverside, she found a leather holster for a gun lying in the weeds. It seemed too small to be for an adult. She wondered if the boy had dropped it. When she got to the riverbank, she saw what the boy had seen, and she didn't for a second think it was a dummy. Snagged on a log was the body of a dark-haired woman, bobbing and weaving with ironic grace in the water, like a barefoot ghost of hair and cloth.

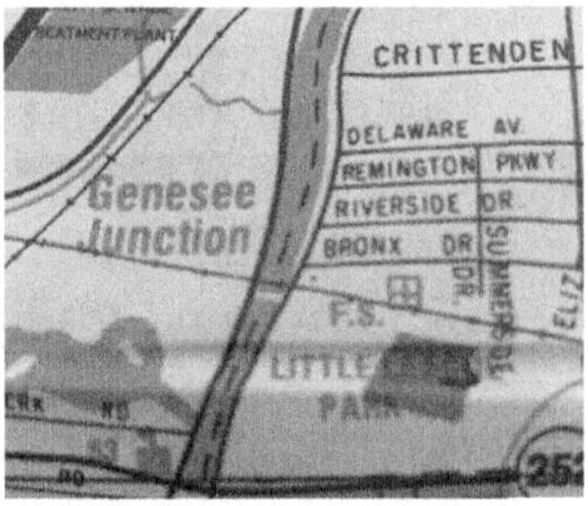

Body was found in the river near the west end of Delaware Ave.

Mrs. Beach no longer ran, but she did return home with quick steps to call the sheriff.

The sheriff's department investigators arrived first, but within an hour the Rochester Police Department (RPD) and Brighton Police also were notified and had detectives at the scene. The banks of the Genesee were searched for the woman's missing shoes and other potential clues. An eight-state alarm was issued, alerting missing-persons investigators.

Morgue Superintendent George Glasser was on scene supervising as the body was hauled up out of the water dripping from the feet and hair, strapped to a stretcher, and carried by hand up the embankment to a waiting morgue ambulance parked on the west shoulder of East River Road.

Just eyeballing the body, the victim appeared to be about thirty years old, and there were visible bullet holes in the upper chest, shoulder area. The body was delivered pronto to the Monroe County Morgue where Coroner Cornelius P. Danehy and Assistant Coroner Floyd S. Winslow performed a thorough autopsy.

The deceased had been apparently healthy in life. Five nine, 140 pounds, brown hair. In the words of the surgeons, she was "proportionately built." She looked much like she had in life, witnesses suspected, except for her hands. What had recently been an elegant hand, finely manicured, now was tipped with nails that were broken and begrimed. There were callouses on her left fingertips. Investigators wondered if perhaps she'd been a seamstress, or maybe a musician.

She had a distinctively long nose, a high forehead, and was wearing a white silk dress with half-inch blue stripes paralleled with skinnier stripes of pink and yellow; a half-inch belt of matching colors, faded pink slip edged with lace, black bra, and pink rayon panties.

She was described as being "strong," with light-brown hair that fell to her shoulders, grayish green eyes, and an "upper face structure indicating possible Slavic blood."

Along with her shoes, also missing was her upper right bicuspid, but apparently from an old extraction and not because of the fatal violence. She had an overbite and the bottom teeth were snaggled.

There was a ten-inch scar along the outside of her left thigh. Dr. Winslow thought she might have been operated on at one point, perhaps for osteomyelitis—although the surgical repair of a compound fracture that had become infected could have caused the same scar.

Investigators noted that pains had been taken to make identification difficult. No shoes, no coat, hat, gloves. No purse. This might have meant she was killed in her own home at a moment when she was not planning to go outside.

Cause of death: gunshot wounds. She'd been shot twice with a .25 caliber automatic pistol. One bullet entered the woman's body at the top of the left shoulder, ranged downward, penetrated a lung and broke three ribs. One of the broken ribs punctured her heart.

The second bullet entered at the right shoulder and also

headed down her body, lodging itself between two lumbar vertebrae.

The path the bullets took was unusual, as if the killer had been above his victim and shot straight down on her. Best guess was that she had been either lying down or bent backward at a sharp angle when shot from behind.

It was murder, all right. There was no way she could have shot herself in this manner.

The woman had been dead between eighteen and twenty hours. Her stomach was empty, indicating that she hadn't eaten for at least five hours before her death.

There was no trace of alcohol in her system. Investigators worked under the theory that the woman had been shot, and then transported by car to be dumped, most likely off the Ballantyne Bridge, about a half-mile upstream.

The Ballantyne Bridge of 1949.

That bridge was south of the spot where the body was found because the Genesee River is one of the few in the Northern Hemisphere that flows northward. (No one considered the possibility that the body had entered the river via Black Creek.)

The Ballantyne Bridge that spanned the river in 1949 was very different in many ways from the one that is there today. For one thing, Jefferson Road and Ballantyne Road didn't line up, and the bridge didn't line up with either one of them.

Heading east on Ballantyne Road, a driver had to take a quick right onto Scottsville Road and then an almost immediate left to get onto the bridge, and you had to be careful if there was a wide load coming in the other direction because the bridge was only about one and three-quarters lanes wide so it was a tight squeeze if two vehicles had to cross paths on the bridge.

The bridge was a black-iron monstrosity, in design a near twin to the trestle that crossed the river just to the north (and is still there). The two bridges remained twins until 1961 when the county tore down the old Ballantyne Bridge, re-routed Jefferson and Ballantyne roads so that one could go from Ballantyne Road, cross the river, and onto Jefferson Road without turning.

The little grocery store Coops that used to be beside Jefferson Road on the east side of the bridge was now and for the rest of its existence down a hill and at the bottom of a driveway from the main road because the road had moved while the store stayed in the same place.

Both bullets were still in the body and so were recovered and turned over to Captain William Winfield and Lieutenant George Keenan of the RPD Identification Bureau.

The bullets had been manufactured by different companies but fired from the same gun. Winfield and Keenan, while at the morgue, fingerprinted the corpse and sent the results to the FBI.

The discovery of the body was first reported to the people of Rochester on the WHAM radio six o'clock news. Television was not yet widespread. That initial report included a description of the woman and the clothes she was wearing.

Sheriff Skinner said the key to solving the murder was to figure out who the victim was. Once her identity was established, he said, the case could be closed in a matter of hours.

The victim's clothes were cheap and casual. She was not gussied up, as one might have expected had the victim been out on a date at the time of her demise. The killer had either abducted her or was familiar enough so that she felt it unnecessary to dress up.

An early lead seemed promising at first, but faded. A man named Roy Lloyd of Shore Drive in East Irondequoit, heard about the discovery of the body and called the Detective Bureau of the Monroe County Sheriff's Office (MCSO) to report a suspicious thing he had seen.

At 9:00 o'clock on Friday night he had watched as a woman got into a car in the trailer camp off Scottsville Road near the airport. Through happenstance he was driving along East River Road near the spot where the body was found, and he saw the *same woman* in a parked car.

Another potential lead came in the form of a suitcase found floating down the river in downtown Rochester near Broad Street. The suitcase was recovered and opened, but contained only paint-smeared worker's clothes, half-filled paint cans, and a large jar of petroleum jelly.

The sheriff announced on Sunday the 24th that anyone who thought they might know who the woman was should come down to the morgue to view the body. Minor repairs were done to the victim's face so she'd better resemble her living self. Astoundingly, over the next two days, six-hundred people showed up, all without a clue as to her identity, all scratching the itch of morbid curiosity.

The body was X-rayed by technician Edward Gunson and specialist Dr. Theodore Steinhauser. They concentrated on the left leg. Hopes were that a bone X-ray would provide a better indication of what had caused her scar.

Since the victim was about thirty years old, and the scar had been inflicted when she was already fully grown, there was also a chance that she might be identified through hospital records.

As it turned out, the X-rays were unnecessary. The identification came on Monday, the 25th, about forty-eight hours after the body's discovery. The FBI matched the fingerprints taken off the body with those of twenty-five year old Jean G.R. Gareis of Oakland, California.

Investigators learned that the victim had been fingerprinted for the first time on October 4, 1942 when applying for a wartime job as a typist with the Monroe Calculating Company in Oakland, California, and then again in June 1943 when applying for a position as a calculating machine operator with the Richmond Ship Yards in Emeryville, California.

As it turned out, Sheriff Skinner, as he so often was, had been correct when he said the I.D. was the key.

A Monroe County deputy sheriff was given the sad duty of calling Jean's parents in Oakland in order to give them the bad news.

The mother wailed, "Jean dead? She can't be! We just got an airmail letter from her."

"How long has it been since you've seen Jean?" the deputy asked.

"Months," the woman said, her voice shaky. "She hasn't lived here for years, since she got married."

"Oh. Who's her husband? Do you have contact information for him?"

"His name is George Hetenyi. I'll get you the address," she said. After a moment she gave the deputy an address in Amherst, New York.

"Do you know his middle name?"

"Paul."

So it was that only hours after the identification police visited the victim's husband. The visit was paid by Deputy Sheriff William Flynn who drove to Buffalo, picked up an escort of Erie County sheriff's deputies, and at 2:30 a.m. knocked urgently at Hetenyi's door.

A paunchy and seemingly sleepy man opened the door, running his thick fingers through an unruly conglomeration of black curls.

"Yes? What do you want at this hour?"

"Is Mrs. Hetenyi here?" Deputy Flynn inquired.

"Don't talk so loud," the sleepy man, his lower lip pushing into a pout. Flynn checked him out. He was tall and husky. "Someone might hear you. No, she's not here. She ran away to her mother in California."

"Afraid not, sir. Your wife is in the Monroe County morgue."

"I don't think so. Anyway, it doesn't interest me. I've nothing to do with it. She left me."

Flynn felt a chill run through him, one that the sleepy man sensed.

"Where are my manners? I mustn't be so inhospitable. Won't you gentlemen come in?"

Flynn shivered again as the man smiled at him, flashing bright white teeth.

"You'd like to ask me a few questions?"

"Yes, sir."

The deputy took a good look at the man and didn't like what he saw. Hetenyi's knuckles were bruised and he had bruises on his face.

"Come in, sit down."

The man sat, the officers remained standing.

"So, when was the last time you saw your wife, Mr. Hetenyi?"

"Reverend. I'm Reverend Hetenyi…I last saw her two nights ago, April twenty-three. I dropped her off at the office of a Buffalo psychiatrist who was treating her. I expected her to come home afterward, but when she didn't I wasn't surprised."

"No?"

"No, she had left me before and was always gone three, four days. You see? I stopped loving her a long time ago. And when she didn't return this time I was sore. That was the last straw. Now I do not care."

"Uh huh. We'd like you to accompany us to Monroe County, city of Rochester, Reverend Hetenyi," Flynn said.

"Why?"

"Two reasons. One thing, we'd like you to identify the body of your wife, and second, the Monroe County District Attorney Anthony Miceli would like to speak with you."

"I will not!" he shouted.

"I fear, sir, that you will have to come with us."

"I am not surrendering my rights. I will not go anywhere until I consult my lawyer."

Hetenyi went to the phone and made a call. (Police later learned that he did not call a lawyer but rather a friend of his who was a special agent for the FBI.)

Hanging up, Hetenyi said, "He tells me to go with you."

Also at home at the time of the raid was the man's mother, seventy-year-old Mrs. Caroline Hetenyi, and George and Jean's two children, two-year-old Diane and nine-month-old Paul.

Investigators quickly learned that Hetenyi was born in Budapest, Hungary in 1909, graduated from the Royal Hungarian Pazmany University, eventually earning a Ph.D. in 1937. A year later, fleeing Hitler, he and his mother Caroline came to Depression-era America.

In the States he studied at Marquette University in Milwaukee, Wisconsin, and at the Pacific School of Religion in Berkeley, California. He came to the States claiming to have been ordained a Catholic priest, and two of his first jobs in America were serving several Roman Catholic Churches with needs for Hungarian-speaking priests.

According to his own legend, he became disenchanted with the Catholic Church, or perhaps his lack of credentials was discovered and he was given the boot. Whichever, he hit the road and became a traveling preacher, setting up his pulpit wherever he could draw a crowd and passing the offertory hat afterwards.

During World War II he was a chaplain for the Defense Council of Churches in the San Francisco Bay area. He served as pastor for churches in Hanny Camp and Pengrove, California, and then for St. Anne's Mission in El Paso, Texas. Following a stint in Texarkana, Texas, he was transferred to a church in the Western New York Episcopal diocese near Batavia, New York (St. Michael's Episcopal Church in Oakfield) during the fall of 1948. Earlier in 1949, Hetenyi was removed as rector at St. Michael's because of complaints about his sometimes-public arguments with his wife.

Initial investigation revealed that, though Hetenyi functioned as an Episcopalian minister, he had never been fully ordained by that church either, but instead worked under what was termed a "special license." As he was no longer participating in church services at the request of the church, he planned to make money writing a series of articles on the history of the Episcopal Church in Western New York State for an Episcopalian newspaper. Hetenyi also claimed to have produced, or was in the process of producing, an "institution and religious directory" covering much of Upstate New York. It was in this capacity that he had visited Rochester several times during the previous year.

When he met his wife in Oakland, California, he was putting it around that he was a minister of the Greek Orthodox Church. After his domestic difficulties earned him removal from the Oakfield, N.Y., church, he continued working for that church in a non-preaching capacity, delivering supplies.

At the time of his arrest, police searched his station wagon, which still had Texas license plates on it and contained a "fully-equipped movable church." There was an organ that was powered by the car's motor, a collapsible altar, and other church appurtenances.

Neighbors in Amherst had never seen the car moved, so it was unknown at first if he'd ever used his mobile church. Later, police learned that Hetenyi had at one time frequently used the church-on-wheels for what he called "street services" but not so much anymore.

Hetenyi was taken to the Detective Division of the Buffalo Police headquarters, and from there to the Monroe County Jail in downtown Rochester. While Hetenyi was being transported eastward, Erie County sheriff's deputies remained at Hetenyi's Amherst house and talked with his mother, who was elderly and nervous about having to take care of the Hetenyis' two small children without any help.

She told police that she couldn't speak to her son's innocence in the death of his wife, that she knew her son took his wife to the psychiatrist on Friday evening, but that she didn't see him again until seven o'clock the next morning.

"I asked him where Jean was and he said she ran away," she offered.

She also admitted that the home had not been a site of marital bliss, ever, really, but especially not lately. Only eleven days before the murder Jean had called the cops complaining that her husband had chased her from the house.

Flynn investigated this incident and learned that the police who answered Jean's call were tentative to take action. Cops didn't like to get involved in domestic squabbles. They talked to the husband and he said, "Pay no attention to my wife. She suffers from a nervous disorder and carries on this way. She nags me to distraction."

After interviewing Hetenyi's mother, Flynn searched the house, paying special attention to the garage. There, he discovered a knife in a sheath, a towel, and suspicious stains on the front-seat upholstery of the car. The car also had a bullet hole in the right-side door and a .25 caliber bullet was still in the hole.

Also in the car Flynn discovered a prayer book inscribed, "May the Good Lord who is present in the Holy Eucharist bless my dear wife, Jean, keep and protect her always, and protect my old mother who raised me to be an ordained priest. Our wedding 8:16:45."

In the car with the suspect were Sheriff Skinner himself, Chief Deputy Ray O'Loughlin, Deputy Sheriff Harry W. McFarland, Superintendent Glasser and Roy Elliot of the *Rochester Democrat & Chronicle* (D&C).

The reporter found Hetenyi to be extremely odd. He was annoyed that police were upsetting his life with all of these trivialities. Most importantly, the reporter thought, Hetenyi did not seem concerned about his wife's death.

On the way, everyone stopped at a coffee shop for breakfast. During the meal, observers were impressed with Hetenyi's suave manners. At one point the Sheriff told Hetenyi that breakfast was on him.

"Oh no, I pay for myself. I'll only let you pay for my funeral," Hetenyi said in an apparent attempt at a joke. No one laughed.

Hetenyi did not eat but drank two cups of black coffee while the Law and the reporter chowed down. He chatted about his career as a preacher, about coming to the U.S. from Europe, and how he considered the U.S. his homeland now. Hungary was just the "old country." When everyone was done eating, he was offered a cigarette but turned it down.

When he got to the sheriff's office in downtown Rochester he complained about the temperature, which he felt was too hot.

After filling in the basics of Hetenyi's biography, investigators went to work on Jean's background. They learned that the victim was born on October 29, 1923, one of seven children, and after a public-school education in Oakland, graduated from the University of California at Berkeley.

She studied to be a concert violinist and played with the Oakland Symphony and then the El Paso Symphony when she went to Texas with her husband. She was married once before to a soldier who was killed in action on Leyte in the Pacific during General Douglas MacArthur's battle for the Philippines.

The Hetenyis had been married for four battle-scarred years. Reports of violent tumult came from neighbors and from Jean's father, William B. Gareis. They told Sheriff Skinner of loud arguments. George frequently threatened his wife.

In March of 1949, the couple moved into the Allenhurst Gardens in Amherst, a complex of semi-attached homes, where there were complaints from neighbors over their violent fights. Frank Sauers of Tonawanda, the super at the Hetenyis' housing complex, told cops about the brouhahas he'd seen and heard.

The couple was last seen by neighbor Mrs. Helen Collins, who said George and Jean got into a car together. George said they were going to a doctor's office. Mrs. Hetenyi was said to have been wearing a bright green coat and a scarf around her head, items that were not found with her body.

Sheriff Skinner was just about to make his move anyway, and then new damning evidence came in. A .25 slug found in Hetenyi's car matched those found in Mrs. Hetenyi. Plus, there had been a clumsy attempt to clean up bloodstains in that garage.

That was all Skinner had to hear.

"Book him," he said.

"Charge?"

"Material witness for now. That'll buy us time."

As Hetenyi was being booked, there was this exchange:

"Occupation?"

"Priest."

"Religion?"

"Episcopalian, but that's next door to Catholic. Make it Catholic."

Out of Hetenyi's earshot, the sheriff was asked, "Should we give his hands a paraffin test?"

"No," Skinner replied. "If he killed her it's too long ago for gun powder to show up on his hands now."

Hetenyi was taken to a Monroe County courtroom where he was remanded by County Judge Daniel J. O'Mara to the County Jail as a material witness in lieu of $50,000 bail. (Equivalent to a half million dollars in today's money.)

During the hearing, Assistant District Attorney (ADA) Harry Rosenthal informed Judge O'Mara that the defendant had been behaving strangely.

"How so, Mr. Rosenthal?" Judge O'Mara inquired.

"He's angry, flies off the handle, broke a window at the jail. I'm afraid that he might not fully comprehend the charge placed against him, your honor," Rosenthal explained.

Judge O'Mara ordered that Hetenyi be taken to the State Hospital where he was to be given a battery of psychological tests to gauge his fitness to participate in his own defense.

Hetenyi had indeed been acting bizarrely. Before court, he was switching from one personality to another like roaming a radio dial looking for the perfect song. His demeanor ranged from relaxed to screaming with anger.

The guys in the jail who were stuck listening to him noticed something about Hetenyi's apparent distress. His screams never had anything to do with the loss of his wife, and everything to do with his own problems. He felt his constitutional rights were abused. He yelled that he was worried about his mother, who was aged and had been left alone with the kids.

He yelled, "I had nothing to do with my wife's death. The last I saw her was on Friday night when I took her to a Buffalo doctor. She left me. She's done it before. Sometimes she's gone for three, four days at a time without a word. I didn't know where she was, and I don't know what happened to her."

His fits of temper grew worse. He went off the deep end in Sheriff Skinner's apartment, which was right down the hall from the jail.

"They won't let me see the bishop. I'll break a window so I can tell the whole world!"

He punched his fist through the window, tipped a potted plant, tried to break a lamp but only left it askew, then overturned a chair before the sheriff and another man physically restrained him. The sheriff was a big man, up and down and all around, and excelled at putting his weight on suspects until they lost the urge to struggle.

Hetenyi cut his already bruised knuckles breaking the window and was given minor medical treatment. He was placed in a cell with bars and under twenty-four-hour surveillance. He would be let out only for his court appearances and a trip to visit the medical examiner.

Despite his earlier refusal to identify the body he was taken to the morgue. Following the physical roughing up he'd gotten after going berserk in Sheriff Skinner's apartment, he was more docile, and although he held his head to one side and for a time refused to look at Jean's body, he eventually relented. He remained highly nervous during the process, and said a brief prayer over his wife.

He muttered, "Jean, Jean," but did not break down, and identified the striped dress as "definitely hers." He noticed two holes in the dress and asked what they were. He was told they were bullet holes, the first mention of any possible gunshots, and upon receiving this info displayed no change in demeanor. He was not told about the bullet and blood found in his garage. Hetenyi had not been in a chatty mood at the morgue anyway, but after he was told about the bullet holes he shut up completely.

Back in Amherst on April 26, Hetenyi's station wagon with its portable altar was transferred to Monroe County where it could be gone over with a fine-tooth comb.

That evening, the victim's sixty-year-old mother, Mrs. William B. Gareis, got on an airplane in Alameda County, California. She touched down at LaGuardia Field in New York City on the morning of the 27th, where there was a layover before she transferred for a flight to Rochester. A reporter greeted her at LaGuardia with pen ready.

The mother said, "Jean was such a good girl, she loved her children so much, I can't understand why this should happen to her." She declined to comment on the murder itself and said she wouldn't until she knew all of the facts.

Officials told reporters the crime took place in Monroe County. Quizzed regarding the precise location of the murder, police had no comment.

"What leads you to believe the crime took place in Monroe County?"

"The evidence that led to the arrest was found in Monroe County."

The determination was important because the location of the murder itself would determine where any eventual trial would take place. With Monroe County taking the ball, Erie County courts were off the hook. Not so, the Erie County Sheriff's Department, whose members would have to testify in Monroe County as to evidence found back home. For now, investigators and crime-scene specialists were still busy searching the Hetenyi home.

The press unearthed some evidence, all from Erie County. There was a service-station proprietor and a dry cleaner who saw Hetenyi doing things he would have difficulty explaining. The witnesses, reporters learned, had been interviewed by a committee of cops representing the MCSO,

RPD, and Amherst police.

The statements were so good that the witnesses were promptly placed under oath and deposed. The dry cleaner was Eli Konikoff of Kenmore who said that on Saturday afternoon, the day following the murder, he was stopped on the street by Hetenyi who handed him a coat that he said needed cleaning. The dry cleaner said it was a woman's coat and there were spots of blood on it. At police instruction, the dry cleaner had brought the coat with him to the deposition.

A second cleaner, Aram Nazarian of Buffalo, told cops that on the Wednesday before the murder Hetenyi dropped off a suit of men's clothes for cleaning. On the day after the murder, Nazarian said, Hetenyi returned to the shop, changed into the cleaned clothes and left the clothes he'd entered in to be cleaned.

"Most folks don't change at the dry cleaners," Nazarian said. "You know, they go home for that part."

Hetenyi's charges were upgraded to murder one at an arraignment in a Monroe County courtroom at 5:40 p.m. on the 27th with Judge O'Mara on the bench. In the courtroom were the accused, the judge, heavy security, eager press, and approximately fifty spectators in the public gallery.

ADA Rosenthal read the charges to Hetenyi as the accused stood between Chief Deputy Ray O'Loughlin and Deputy Robert Fagan. He was informed at this time of his rights to obtain counsel (this was long before the days of Miranda).

Hetenyi said that he had been asking ever since he was arrested as a material witness that he wanted attorney William B. Mahoney of Buffalo to represent him, but he had still not had an opportunity to speak to Mahoney. He again lost his composure and complained to Undersheriff George Conway that his constitutional rights were being "stepped on as if by storm troopers.

"I'm not even allowed to look at the newspapers! What are you guys trying to pull here?"

He couldn't control his anger—but he lacked grief. As he demonstrated his discontent, he turned his back to Judge O'Mara and played to the spectators and press.

"Reverend Hetenyi, please stop. Do you have sufficient funds to hire an attorney?" Judge O'Mara asked.

Turning his back to the judge, Hetenyi said, "Your honor, I have spoken with Bishop Lauriston L. Scaife of the Western New York Episcopal Diocese and he said the diocese will provide funds for my defense." (It later turned out that no such assurance had taken place and the church had no intention of giving a dime to Hetenyi's cause.)

After court, Hetenyi was placed in a jail cell and was allowed to call Mahoney. The call lasted several minutes and when it ended Hetenyi angrily slammed the receiver back on the hook.

Because Hetenyi had interests in the case that might have undervalued the truth, Jean's mother was taken to the morgue to identify her daughter, for corroboration.

As she viewed the body, Mrs. Gareis said, "My dear child, my poor baby," before breaking down. She was hustled back to Sheriff Skinner's apartment, which was already straightened up and the window fixed after Hetenyi's disruptive outburst.

On her way out of the morgue a reporter asked if she had any feeling about her daughter's husband.

"With all my heart," she replied, "I wanted Jean to wait and think more about it before she married the Reverend Hetenyi. They were married three or four months after they first met."

Her voice still had a touch of an accent. She's been born in Hamburg, Germany and didn't come to the United States until she was eighteen years old.

"How did they meet?"

"In the office of a San Francisco food broker where Jean was a secretary, four years ago this coming August. I wanted them to wait so badly. Jean was so broken up by the death of her first husband in the service and she wanted to do good in the world. My daughter was a very religious person. She used to teach Sunday school. She was only twenty-one when she married Hetenyi. I felt he was too old for her."

She added that she would do whatever she could to help authorities solve the crime but refused to pass judgment on Hetenyi. She said that she had never seen her youngest grandchild, not even a photo. She had asked repeatedly for a photo of little Paul, but none ever arrived. She'd last seen Jean in January 1948 when she visited her daughter and family in El Paso. She had planned to visit Jean and meet the new baby later that spring.

"Have you thought about the children's future?"

"I cannot say anything about that. Mr. Hetenyi is their father, after all. I would be glad to have them. My husband and I both love children and we have a home in the country."

"Hetenyi says your daughter was under a psychiatrist's care."

"As far as I know, she never had any need for that. It must have been his idea."

Miss Anna Skinner, the sheriff's sister and jail matron, prepared lunch for Mrs. Gareis during her visit to the sheriff's apartment. Before she left she thanked both the sheriff and his sister for their hospitality: "You have all been wonderful. Everyone has, and I am grateful."

There were questions over what to do with the victim's body. Morgue Superintendent Glasser came to Hetenyi on the morning of the 27th with a release form, allowing him to turn the body over to an undertaker.

"No way," Hetenyi said. "I want the body to remain in the morgue until this matter is disposed of."

Glasser thought Hetenyi was out of touch with reality, in denial, but there was nothing he could do for the time being.

Sheriff Skinner was lauded for the quick arrest, but he said the thanks should be spread around: "I want everyone who had a hand in the case to know that I am most grateful for the tremendous help given us. I cannot list the names of city, town, county, and out-of-the-county officials who helped us, but I do want them to know that the work was wonderful. This includes the hundreds of citizens who helped out by trying to identify the body of Mrs. Hetenyi while we still had a seemingly unsolvable mystery on our hands. It was all real cooperation."

Those close to the sheriff said that he was operating without sleep, that he'd been up and on the case from the moment he heard of the body being found in the river.

Hearing about Hetenyi's refusal to release the body, Jean's mother said that she would take care of funeral arrangements if Hetenyi would permit her. He wouldn't, so she got on another plane, her third in two days, and flew to Buffalo where she went to the Hetenyi home and helped Hetenyi's mother take care of the kids. At no time during her visit to

Sheriff Skinner

Rochester had she seen Hetenyi, and that was fine with her.

Hetenyi, after discussing the matter with his own mother, decided something had to be done with Jean's body, so he sent a message to his mother-in-law saying she could make arrangements if she chose—although he insisted upon veto power over anything he didn't like.

Police learned that Hetenyi had been telling the truth when he said he took his wife to a doctor on the day before she died. Investigators talked to the psychiatrist who said he couldn't talk about her condition except as it perhaps pertained to her murder, but he'd have to think about that. He said that she had not made an appointment for a future visit, which he thought odd, but he did hear from her again.

"When?" police asked.

"That evening sometime."

"Can you discuss what she wanted?"

"Sure, she said she had lost her watch and she wondered if she'd left it in my office. I said no, I'd found no watch and that was that."

With Jean's mom watching the kids, George Hetenyi's mother, seventy-year-old Caroline Hetenyi, was free on April 28 to travel from Amherst to visit her son in jail.

She appeared feeble to the sheriff's deputies, one of whom had her by the arm every time she moved from one place to another. She needed a deputy at each arm to help her up a small set of stairs in the jail block, and delivered to her son a set of fresh clerical clothes.

"My poor boy," she was overheard saying as she took him in her arms. He gave her a list of other clothes and items he needed from his Amherst home and the slight woman put on her glasses to read it.

After her visit she told a reporter than she didn't understand what all of this was about, that her son was always "a first-class boy."

"Why did you come to America from Hungary back in 1938?"

"We wanted to get away from the Germans," she replied in a clipped tone.

His mother was not Hetenyi's only visitor that day. Hetenyi's earlier attempts to get a lawyer named William Mahoney to represent him had fallen through. So he tried again. Two lawyers—John S. McGovern and Maurice Goldman of Buffalo—met with the prisoner on the 28th and on the way out told a reporter that they would decide if they were going to take Hetenyi's case in "a few days."

Also on April 28 Mrs. Clara Beach called the sheriff about the holster she'd found just before she saw the body in the river.

The sheriff came to pick up the evidence and realized the holster's importance right away. It was built for a .25, the type of gun that killed Jean Hetenyi.

"Where exactly did you find it, Mrs. Beach?" Sheriff Skinner asked.

"It was in the weeds about six feet off the shoulder of East River Road and about fifty feet south of the body." She had pondered the carelessness of the holster's owner. "It's a very odd thing to lose," she recalled thinking at the time.

Mrs. Beach explained that the holster was so tiny that she thought it was for a child, for a toy gun. Skinner didn't think it looked much like part of a child's cowboy costume. It was handmade of finely tooled leather.

Mrs. Beach's judgment aside, the location at which the holster was found was key. Police hoped that the killer had chucked the gun into the river close to the spot where he dropped the holster.

The riverbed near that spot was scanned by two men in a rowboat with an electromagnet with negative results. The searchers couldn't make a gun materialize, but they created traffic jams on both sides of the river, curiosity seekers clogging both East River Road and Scottville Road. In those days, before expressways, both roads were popular routes to get to neighboring towns to the south, Henrietta and Wheatland.

On the second day of the river search, the sheriff made an impassioned plea to motorists to avoid the area. There really wasn't anything interesting to see, and law enforcement didn't want to be held responsible for those who were behind schedule because they had the misfortune of driving very slowly past the search site.

There was less traffic on the final day of the magnet search, but no greater results. In the afternoon water-soaked cables caused the metal-detector to go on the fritz and the search was temporarily abandoned.

Hetenyi went on another outing on Sunday, May 1—a big deal for a man living in a cage. Cuffed, and with Chief Deputy O'Loughlin on his arm, Hetenyi was removed from his cell during the late afternoon and led down the hallway to attend religious services in an assembly room at the rear of the jail, services performed by the Reverend Domenico A. Porfirio.

Hetenyi wore his Sunday best: spruce black suit and white clerical collar. From the neck down he looked pretty sharp. From the neck up he looked worn and unkempt. Hetenyi hadn't shaved and his five-day beard painted a vagrant's shadow upon his jowls.

Sheriff Skinner later explained that, because of the prisoner's perhaps delicate mental state, he was not allowed to shave himself. Sheriff Skinner had offered him the services of the jail barber and Hetenyi had declined.

"Don't you at least want to be clean-shaven for your wife's funeral?" Sheriff Skinner asked.

"I will do as I see best," Hetenyi said.

Hetenyi was not allowed to get within arm's reach of anyone else at the service. In fact, he was told to sit in a chair that had been dragged back into the doorway. For reasons unknown, Hetenyi did not make himself comfortable and perched himself on the very front edge of the chair as if he feared the seat was soiled or something. The trustee distributing the clothbound prayer books did not give the book directly to Hetenyi. He gave the book to O'Loughlin who gave it to the Hetenyi. According to O'Loughlin, Hetenyi was very nervous throughout the prayer service, and though he followed along in the prayer book, during the hymns he did not sing along with the other inmates.

Hetenyi didn't know it, but his former mother-in-law was back in Rochester, in fact right down the hall accompanied by Jean's sister, Mrs. Elsie Steele of Rittman, Ohio. Mrs. Gareis told Sheriff Skinner that she was in Rochester to complete arrangements for Jean's funeral. The woman wanted the sheriff to know the details, as a certain amount of security was necessary, considering the notoriety of the case, and all of the strong emotions involved.

Yet another witness had emerged, a guy named Lee Rovall, a forty-six-year-old machine operator for a Buffalo industrial plant. He approached police over the weekend. He said he saw Hetenyi and his wife while waiting for a bus at a Buffalo intersection on the Friday night before Jean's death.

"What time?" police asked.

"About eight."

Police asked Rovall why he hadn't come forward with his information earlier. Rovall replied that he "didn't want to get mixed up in the case."

Police didn't like it, but they still wanted to hear his story.

Rovall said that he recognized Hetenyi from his picture in the paper. When he saw him near the bus stop he was dressed in clerical garb and pacing back and forth nervously.

"What made the guy so memorable?"

"He approached me and began talking in a monologue," Rovall said. This odd duck was suddenly filibustering to a complete stranger.

"What did he talk about?"

"He said he had a wife who was ill. Sick in the head. He'd taken her to a series of psychiatrists but none of them did no good. He said one psychiatrist was a quack who told him he was the one who should seek help, not his wife."

Rovall remembered thinking that wasn't the worst idea he'd ever heard.

"The guy said he had been abused by his wife and he was at his wit's end."

It got weirder. Rovall was there to catch the bus, but when the bus came and Rovall stepped toward the curb, the clergyman stepped in front of him and waved the bus on.

"I guess he didn't want me to leave and interrupt him in the middle of his speech," Rovall said.

Surprisingly, Rovall didn't get angry at this, and continued to engage with the talkative minister. Rovall said that he was personally acquainted with a medical doctor with a specialty in psychiatry and the clergyman seemed very interested in getting the doctor's name.

Police wanted to know where the man's wife was during this conversation. Rovall said that she was there for part of it and for part she walked away and was inside a nearby drug store for a few minutes.

"Could you write the doctor's name on a piece of paper?" the clergyman asked, while his wife was out of earshot.

Rovall did so. It was at that point that the man's wife came out of the drug store and approached them at the bus stop. Seeing his wife approach, the clergyman snatched the piece of paper out of Rovall's hand and shoved it in his pocket.

"I saw the picture of the poor murdered woman in the papers. It was her all right, and it was him too. No doubt in my mind."

"What happened then?"

"The wife walked across the street and got into the passenger side of a parked car. The clergyman followed her and got behind the wheel. They drove away. I couldn't believe it. The guy never said thank you or good bye or anything, and the thing that irked me was he wasn't even waiting for the bus!"

Rochesterians were hungry for details regarding the minister and his wife. Newspaper sales rose sharply. As the new workweek began, there was news of a mystery witness who, according to ADA Clarence J. Henry, had seen Hetenyi in Rochester at midnight, only hours before his wife's body was discovered. Authorities kept the witness's identity a secret, but wanted the public to know Hetenyi was in town that night, and not in Amherst as he claimed busy not caring that his wife had run away again.

Investigators had known since early on that Hetenyi was lying about his whereabouts on the night before Jean was found. But they'd kept a lid on that info until after Hetenyi was arraigned.

Further details leaked: The witness had walked into the Monroe County jail on Tuesday night. He told the sheriff that he'd seen the photo of Hetenyi in the morning paper and recognized him as a man he saw on the night of the murder. He said that around midnight, Friday night, he was walking in front of the City Hall Annex at the west end of the Court Street bridge, when a tan 1947 sedanette, driven by a clergyman, stopped and the driver hailed him. The witness said it was Hetenyi all right and he asked a series of fascinating questions, questions the witness thought odd even at the time but became sinister with later revelations. Hetenyi, the witness said, wanted to know the depth of the raceway that ran between the City Hall Annex and the Salvation Army Hotel and warehouse.

"How do I get to the upper stretches of the river, south of the city?" the clergyman asked.

The witness gave him directions involving East River Road.

"Anyone else in the car?"

"No, sir."

Sheriff Skinner asked, "Would you recognize the car again if you saw it?"

The witness said he would, so the sheriff took him to the Monroe County garage, where they'd towed Hetenyi's mobile-church station wagon from Amherst.

"That's it," the witness said. He recognized the wired defrosting device on the left front windshield, and the stickers in the lower left corner of the windshield. Upon closer examination, those stickers were from the Texas Motor Vehicle Bureau.

From there the witness was taken to Sheriff Skinner's apartment. The prisoner was brought in.

"That's him," the witness said.

"What is this? Gestapo?" Hetenyi asked angrily.

On April 29, Sheriff Skinner got into a car with ADA Henry, a few MCSO crime-scene investigators, and a RPD chemist, and headed for Amherst to see what evidence they could find at the Hetenyi home.

Skinner wouldn't be specific about the mission but assured Rochesterians that he would be back in the Flower City by day's end. Secretly, they had the gun holster with them. There was a green stain on the holster and they wanted to see if they could match it up with paint at the Hetenyi home.

The search went on for a few hours but they came back with sad faces. No matching paint had been found.

The chemist was asked for an update and said that there "was nothing new to report." The chemist's next job was to go out to the river and Delaware Avenue to check red blotches on a guardrail cable along East River Road. These were quickly determined not to be bloodstains.

As this was going on, the same two workers in a rowboat who'd failed with the electromagnet now dragged the river in the area where Jean's body was found. Morgue Superintendent Glasser supervised the work.

There were mature trees growing out of the east bank of

the river and stretching out over the water, closer to horizontal than vertical, looking as if they might fall into the water at any second.

Asked what they were looking for, they said the victim's coat, scarf, and shoes and the killer's .25 caliber gun—and anything else they might find.

All they found was a cardboard box containing a pair of red gloves. They bagged it for evidence but they were not optimistic that it had anything to do with their murder case.

Jean's remains were finally moved from the county morgue to the Thomas Honan funeral parlor at the corner of Genesee and Magnolia streets.

According to police sources, Hetenyi originally said he wanted the funeral in Oakfield. But police couldn't find a local undertaker there and asked Hetenyi for his second choice.

Hetenyi said, "The guy at the morgue who embalmed Jean did a good job, maybe he could take care of it."

And that was how Honan got the job.

Honan and Hetenyi were allowed to have a brief conversation. Hetenyi told Honan that he wanted an Episcopalian clergyman to preside over the ceremony so Honan set about to make that happen.

On April 29, the Associated Press reported that a letter from the victim, postmarked the day after her death, had been delivered to her parents' home. Jean's father, William Gareis, told the wire service reporter that the letter was unusual. He'd received many letters from his daughter and knew that she always hand wrote the address on the envelope. On this letter, for the first time, the Oakland address had been typed.

Sheriff Skinner examined the letter and said that, other than the envelope being different, the letter seemed ordinary enough. There was nothing in it regarding Jean's marriage. The letter's news was mundane, and as far as the sheriff could tell there was nothing there that might be considered evidentiary—except of course for the fact that someone had mailed it the day after she died. An attempt had been made to make it look as if Jean had lived longer than she had.

On April 30, the MCSO released information regarding three pieces of what they termed a "tightening noose of circumstantial evidence." A new witness said she saw Hetenyi in Rochester on the Friday night before Jean's body was found. She was a waitress at a downtown Rochester restaurant who would swear that she saw Hetenyi at 11:30 p.m. on that Friday evening. She said he came in alone and ordered a drink and a plate of spaghetti. She remembered him in particular because he was dressed in clerical garb and yet ordered hard liquor, which was a first to her knowledge. She kept an eye on him. He drank his drink, barely touched his spaghetti, paid his bill, and left. He didn't seem nervous or anything, just like a man who had unexpectedly lost his appetite. The waitress's identity was being kept a secret by the district attorney's office, so no efforts could be made to intimidate her.

Number two was discovery of a blood-soaked piece of cloth just off Jefferson Road near the Ballantyne Bridge, a half-mile south of where the body was found. The name of the person who found the cloth was also kept a secret by the D.A. That guy hand-delivered the potential evidence to RPD Chief Vincent Conklin. The chief called the sheriff to report the finding and found Skinner and a crew of others about to depart for Amherst to look for green paint. The cloth was added to the Sheriff's agenda. While in Amherst they would check to see if there was any cloth in the Hetenyi's home that was identical to that found bloodstained near the bridge. Chemist Don A. Temmerman examined the cloth and concluded that the blood was human, but no similar cloth was found at the Hetenyi's home.

The third item was the previously mentioned letter from Jean to her parents. The sheriff planned to compare the typewriting on the envelope to the typewriters in the Hetenyi home. Sometimes the letter elements on typewriters had imperfections so that items typed on that machine could be linked to that typewriter to the exclusion of all other typewriters. Skinner asked Hetenyi if he had a typewriter and he admitted that he had, a portable that he kept at the house. He wanted to know why the subject had come up, but the sheriff revealed nothing.

District Attorney Miceli was talking tough, giving reporters usable quotes, like: "What appeared to be a perfect crime turned out to be a plain case of murder, first degree. The sheriff, police, FBI, morgue officials, the coroner and his medical examiners, city officials, press and radio, and the district attorney's office were at each other's beck and call to solve the case. I never before experienced such teamwork in gathering evidence to solve a crime and I am grateful to all of them. My main concern now is what to do with the Reverend George Hetenyi. If it develops that he is insane, I will ask for an order to commit him to Matteawan State Hospital. But if he is found not to be insane, he will be vigorously prosecuted for the murder of his wife. The case, however, will be presented to the grand jury which reconvenes May 9."

So it was all sewed up. Almost. As Miceli gave his case-closed speech to reporters, the Reverend George Hetenyi still didn't have an attorney. He was all alone and no one was his friend.

Sheriff Skinner hinted at witnesses whose statements had not yet been made public. He said that although he had witnesses to Hetenyi being in Rochester on the evening before the murder, there was also eyewitness evidence that this was not the first time that the clergyman had visited the Flower City.

Detectives in Buffalo located a bank at which Hetenyi had attempted to do business on April 25, 1949.

Upon entering, Hetenyi had said, "I'd like to rent a safety deposit box."

"Sorry, there are none available at the moment," a bank

rep replied.

Hetenyi then did an odd and thoroughly memorable thing: "I want you to take this envelope and deliver it for me," Hetenyi said.

"That would seem to be the post office's job, sir," said the confused bank rep.

"I need it to go to my mother in case anything should happen to me."

Hetenyi gave the man the envelope and quickly left the bank. Interestingly, not knowing what was in the envelope, it was decided to keep the envelope safe by locking it inside the bank's main vault.

When Hetenyi's name came up in the paper accused of murdering his wife, someone from the bank retrieved the envelope from the vault and called the Erie County district attorney.

The D.A. said the vault was a good place for the envelope, and expressed no immediate interest in seeing it. Instead, he said that he would request that the envelope be brought to him if and when it was deemed necessary evidence to successfully prosecute Hetenyi.

He then called the Erie County sheriff to tell him about the envelope. The sheriff in turn sent Undersheriff Arthur S.C. Loepere to examine the unopened envelope. He found that the envelope was flat and could not contain the missing murder weapon—apparently the only immediate concern. The letter remained unopened.

The psychiatrist assigned to examine Hetenyi on behalf of the people of Monroe County was Dr. Richard C. Jaenike, assistant professor of psychiatry at the University of Rochester/Strong Memorial Hospital. Dr. Jaenike functioned as a psychiatric aide for city and county authorities.

If Jaenike diagnosed mental illness, a judge could commit Hetenyi to the Rochester State Hospital for another series of examinations by a "sanity board." The board would report their findings back to the court and the law would have the option of committing Hetenyi to a state hospital supervised by the State Department of Mental Hygiene, such as Rochester State, or to Matteawan State Hospital operated by the state's Department of Correction. The commitment, interestingly, did not depend on a jury finding Hetenyi guilty of murdering his wife.

On May 3, Jean's funeral was held and, as expected, the now clean-shaven Rev. George Hetenyi stole the show. He was the one the crowd was there to see, and boy was there a crowd.

The case had touched a nerve in Rochester and everyone wanted to get a glimpse of the preacher who offed his wife. An estimated eight-hundred persons showed up.

During the day, Hetenyi remained composed for the most part, only losing it once as he entered St. Andrew Episcopal Church, at Averill Avenue and Ashland Street, just off Mount Hope Avenue in the South Wedge section of the city. The church, known for its high altar and bell tower, was built of brick and stone in the 1870s in Gothic Revival style.

Hetenyi was handcuffed on either side to deputies Fagan and O'Loughlin. Just before entering the church he stopped and shivered violently. Then he composed himself and managed to walk without interruption to his front pew.

Officiating was the Rt. Rev. Lauriston L. Scaife, bishop of the Western New York Episcopal Diocese. The ceremony was simple but solemn. Hetenyi kept his chin up. He very formally followed the actions of the mass. After a time, the other mourners bored of looking at him and stared straight ahead in their own emotional and spiritual space.

In the front pew, Hetenyi was uncuffed from the deputies and his hands were recuffed together in front of him so he could pray. Each time Hetenyi folded his hands in prayer he audibly clanked his handcuffs together.

St. Andrew Episcopal Church

Burial was at Riverside Cemetery. Jean would reside for eternity beside the river in which her body was found. The procession from church to grave was very short: Jean's hearse, followed by a limo containing her mother and sister Elsie.

Jean's mom was dressed in a tailored cocoa brown colored suit with a print blouse, gold and brown wool knit beret, black shoes, gloves and bag. She sat apart from the Hetenyi clan and never spoke. She was already in the funeral parlor when Hetenyi came in handcuffed to the deputies and she covered her face with her hands rather than look at him.

Surprisingly, it was Hetenyi's mom Caroline who wailed the loudest at the graveside. Dressed in a black coat and hat, black shoes, black handbag, black gloves, handkerchief in hand, she had kept her composure throughout the day at the funeral parlor and church, mostly staring at the floor with a blank expression, moving from one place to another when told to do so, but next to the hole in the ground she began to sob loudly. When her knees threatened to buckle, she was helped by Sheriff Skinner on one side and Lester Steele, the victim's brother-in-law, on the other.

After prayers at the gravesite, Caroline grabbed Bishop Scaife by the elbow and was overheard saying, "My boy told me he didn't do it. I know he didn't do it. Please help him."

She repeatedly kissed the bishop's hand until it clearly made him uncomfortable.

"We will do all that we can," the bishop said, finally pulling his hand free.

Hetenyi was given the option of leaving after the words or staying to see his wife lowered into the grave. Hetenyi said he wanted to stick around. This caused logistical problems. Police put Hetenyi in a car and drove him away. They waited until the hundreds of spectators had left and then returned Hetenyi to the grave alone to be with his wife's casket as it was lowered.

They uncuffed him for a moment during this process and gave him some space, but not too much space. Police kept a close ear on the defendant, just in case he wanted to apologize to his dead wife for anything.

When Hetenyi had finished at Jean's graveside, he was recuffed to the two deputies and taken back to jail where, while he was in a quiet mood, Sheriff Skinner asked him what was in the sealed envelope that he'd mysteriously taken to the bank.

"Important papers," Hetenyi said. "Insurance policies, personal papers, things like that."

May 4 was a hot day in Rochester with the temperature hitting ninety-one degrees, a record for the date, and the day before Hetenyi was to receive his court-ordered mental examination. Dr. Jaenike had already preliminarily interviewed Hetenyi a couple of times and said that the clergyman was "suffering from a serious personality condition and showed emotional instability with many paranoid trends and possible delusions."

He found Hetenyi to be evasive and on the defensive, a man who wanted to avoid being candid, a man who had secrets he didn't want to tell. The evasiveness was selective rather than across the board. He had no trouble talking about his life, and even the troubles he'd been having with his wife, but the closer the topic got to the night of his wife's death, the less he wanted to say.

Dr. Jaenike's notes and theories regarding his interviews with the defendant were written in an affidavit to ADA Rosenthal. Dr. Jaenike recommended that the "paranoid reactions to the defendant's predicament and to his wife's death all indicate the existence of a mental condition and the need for further examination and observation."

There were grounds, the psychiatrist continued, to believe that the defendant was in "such a state of insanity that he may be incapable of understanding the charge or proceeding or of making his defense."

Close observers of Hetenyi and his captors since his arrest had noticed a steady increase in the security around the defendant whenever he was outside his jail cell. During his first two court appearances, first as a material witness and then the next day when he was charged with first-degree murder, only one guard accompanied him. He was handcuffed to the guard when in transit but the handcuffs were removed when he was in the courtroom. For his wife's funeral, Hetenyi was double fettered.

On this hot Wednesday, his ninth in jail, as Hetenyi was taken to court for his arraignment hearing, he again was cuffed to two deputies, one on either side.

The court hearing again was brief. Judge O'Mara asked if Hetenyi had a lawyer yet and the defendant said no. "I have conferred with a number of lawyers, your honor, and am waiting to hear back about whether they will take my case."

Hearing that, Judge O'Mara granted the defendant another week's adjournment.

On the evening of May 5, Hetenyi was transported from

the jail to the State Hospital. The following morning his sanity tests began. The psychiatrists assigned to the case were Dr. O. Arnold Kilpatrick, the director of the Rochester State Hospital, and Drs. Harold Feldman and Benjamin Pollack. Dr. Kilpatrick estimated that the tests would take about two weeks. When the tests were through the doctors would write up their reports and submit them to Judge O'Mara.

Rochester State Hospital

On Tuesday, May 10, the Monroe County Grand Jury met in the downtown Rochester courthouse and began hearing evidence in the murder of Jean Hetenyi. D.A. Miceli had subpoenaed about thirty witnesses and was hoping to examine all of them in two days. As grand jury proceedings are secret, no names were released and no testimony became public. Considering all of that secrecy, it's odd that the daily newspapers published the name of the grand jury foreman, Leo L. Fredericks, and even mentioned his address: 320 Washington Avenue in Irondequoit. When he wasn't leading grand juries, the paper said, Mr. Fredericks was a welder.

On May 19, 1949, at Hetenyi's indictment hearing, psychiatrists at the state hospital proclaimed Hetenyi sane and fit to stand trial. The diagnosis was that, though the subject was anchored in reality, he spent part of his time in a "dream world." His biggest psychological issue was anger management, doctors said. No surprise there.

At the hearing, Hetenyi told Judge O'Mara that his search for a lawyer had been unsuccessful. Those he'd contacted either said they didn't want the case or were too expensive.

Hearing that, Judge O'Mara appointed George J. Skivington of Scottsville (7 Rochester Street) to represent Hetenyi, a fact that delighted reporters.

From a journalistic point of view, the white-haired Skivington was fun to cover. He was a master of the courtroom and had a reputation for the dramatic and unexpected—a real life Perry Mason. (The big difference was Mason's clients were *always* innocent. Skivington was not so lucky.)

Skivington rolled up his sleeves and went to work immediately, making two demands:

One: he wanted authorities to inform him precisely where and when the murder of Jean Hetenyi took place.

Two: he wanted the court to spend $1000 so he could hire two defense psychiatrists. Without doctors of his own, he maintained, he wouldn't properly be able to cross-examine the prosecution's doctors.

The first answer to Skivington's first demand was that the prosecution did not know when and where the murder took place. The second answer was yes, and Skivington got his defense doctors to help counter the prosecution psychiatrists' testimony.

On November 1, 1949, at a court hearing, Skivington demonstrated that he was going to make a major issue out of the unknown location of the crime. He would mention the prosecution's ignorance relentlessly. He wanted Judge O'Mara to *compel* the prosecution to name the place and time of the crime. The indictment, as it was written, said that the murder took place "on or about" April 22, 1949 in the County of Monroe." That wasn't good enough, Skivington argued.

Jury selection for the trial took place during the autumn. The court ordered a pool of 150 prospective jurors be drawn, but Skivington took exception to the pool.

The defense attorney said, "The jury commissioner discriminates against the common, working people, persons of foreign birth—particularly the large so-called Italian population of the City of Rochester—and against Negroes."

Skivington challenged the notion of a "Blue-Ribbon Jury," which was code for "all white men." No one had ever gone after Monroe County's jury system in this manner before, and there was considerable outrage.

On December 3, 1949, Judge O'Mara disallowed the challenge. Jury selection began on December 5, and twelve jurors and two alternates were chosen over the next three days.

Skivington couldn't have been happy. He ended up getting precisely the jury he'd feared the most, a stern yet upstanding panel of Republicans. There were two women on the jury, a positive, but the ladies seemed pretty Republican as well.

The trial took place in the building that became known as the County Office Building on Main Street and quickly earned a reputation as the best show in town. Every day there was a line out of the door of citizens who wanted to be lucky enough to sit in the gallery. Many were turned away. A second shorter line formed mid-day in hopes of occupying seats vacated by mornings-only spectators.

District Attorney Clarence Henry sat behind the prosecution desk. George Skivington was joined at the defense table by his son, George Jr., and the defendant. Hetenyi's entrance caught some by surprise. He was wearing his clerical robes and strutted proudly to the defense table where he dramatically sat and opened a prayer book in front of him. He seemed zoned in on the book even as there was movement all around him and didn't snap out of it until his mother put her arms around him and kissed him. She then moved stiffly to her seat, taking a quick glance at the prosecution table as she went. Hetenyi's mom would be a constant fixture in the courtroom throughout the trial.

The defendant's mom wasn't the only one looking at the prosecution table, which was set up for show-and-tell. On and about that table were an odd assortment of items including a black clerical robe, the holster found off East River Road, a towel, and bullets.

Hetenyi kept his eyes on his book, cupping his left hand under his chin as he read so that the jury could get a good look at what spectators called his "fat gold wedding ring."

More evidence was carted into the courtroom, including some cumbersome items that were placed in front of the prosecution's table. They were parts of an automobile: a door panel, floor mat and bench seat.

The jury entered last, and solemnly took their seats in the jury box.

Judge O'Mara said, "Mr. Henry, are you ready to make your opening statement?"

"Yes, your honor," the D.A. replied.

Henry told the jury about Hetenyi's "peripatetic life," his temper issues, his rocky career as a so-called man of the cloth, ranging wildly from working as a Catholic priest to a stint in 1944 California as a fly-by-night preacher.

"He offered sermons to rural folk from his mobile station-wagon church," Henry said.

Hetenyi kept his nose in his prayer book as the prosecutor patiently itemized for the jury all of the ways Hetenyi mistreated his wife.

"You'll hear testimony to support each and every item," Henry promised.

Judge O'Mara asked Skivington if he would be addressing the jury.

"We'll defer our opening statement until after the prosecution's case, your honor," Skivington said.

"Mr. Henry, call your first witness," Judge O'Mara said.

"The people call to the stand Leslie McMahon," Henry said.

A bailiff went down the middle aisle to the door, and opened it for McMahon, who to the amusement of some was a little kid. Looking slightly spooked, he testified that he'd gone fishing on the Saturday morning in question, saw the body in the river between 9:30 and 10:00 a.m., and initially thought it was a dummy. There was no cross-examination and Leslie was out of there in under fifteen minutes.

"People call Mrs. Clara Beach."

Ms. Beach entered the courtroom on steady enough legs, but with eyes that shifted from here to there, taking in everything without focusing on anything.

Mrs. Beach testified that she had first discovered a small gun holster. After that she saw a boy who'd been fishing and had seen "something funny," and then the body of the victim.

"Other than the body in the river, did you find anything else that morning?"

"Objection, relevance," Skivington said.

"Overruled."

"Yes, I found a holster for a small caliber gun."

"Is this that holster?" Henry said, holding it up.

"Yes."

"Your honor, I move to enter the holster into evidence."

"Objection, your honor. There is nothing to connect this holster to this defendant or this case."

"Overruled."

Skivington declined to cross-examine the witness.

"Witness is excused," Judge O'Mara said.

Mrs. Beach took a deep breath and exited the courtroom eyes ahead, without looking from side to side. She couldn't wait to get out of the courtroom and into the hall again so she could once again breathe properly.

"People call Sheriff's Deputy William Flynn."

Deputy Flynn testified as to the defendant's chilly demeanor when he woke him up and informed him that his wife was dead. He testified that he searched Hetenyi's garage and there discovered the defendant's car with a bullet hole in its door.

Rochester chemist Don A. Temmerman took the stand and testified that he had tested stains on the auto seat from Hetenyi's station wagon, as well as items found inside the car and on the sleeve of one of Hetenyi's clerical robes.

"Did you determine what those stains were?"

"Yes, sir. They were human blood."

Temmerman said that he found blood at eleven locations on the seat, as well as on a towel and sleeve. The towel and the robe had revealed blood drops despite the fact that there was also the presence of cleaning fluid at those spots.

"An attempt had been made to remove the bloodstains?" Henry asked.

"Objection, your honor. Question calls for a conclusion," Skivington said.

"Sustained," Judge O'Mara said.

"You found both traces of human blood and cleaning fluid on the car seat?" Henry asked.

"Yes, sir."

"No further questions," said Henry.

"Cross-examination, Mr. Skivington?" Judge O'Mara said.

"Yes. Thank you, your honor. Mr. Temmerman, did you type Mrs. Hetenyi's blood?" Skivington queried.

"I did not," Temmerman replied.

"Then you cannot say whether the blood on the articles is Mrs. Hetenyi's blood, is that correct?"

"I cannot."

"No further questions."

"Witness is excused," Judge O'Mara said. "Call your next witness, Mr. Henry."

"The people call Lieutenant George William Keenan."

Keenan was sworn in and told the court that he was an RPD ballistics expert, that he had examined the bullets recovered in the body and the bullet recovered in the door of the defendant's station wagon, and that he could conclusively say that they had all been fired from the same gun.

"Bullets fired from the same gun match up like a Chinese laundry ticket," Keenan testified.

Skivington grinned when he heard that. His first question on cross-examination was, "Then you compared these bullets with one you fired from the defendant's gun?"

"No, sir."

"No? Why not?"

"We couldn't find the defendant's gun," Keenan said.

The victim's mother was called to the witness stand. She testified in a quiet voice that Jean was one of seven children, that her daughter was very accomplished for a still-young woman. She was a concert violinist, a Sunday school teacher, a Rosie the Riveter type woman who had worked during the war in an Oakland shipyard.

Jean fell in love and married a sailor named Milton Vickery, who was subsequently killed in action during the Battle of Leyte Gulf. Now a devastated young widow, she looked at no man for a full year. Then Hetenyi drove into the shipyard in that mobile church station wagon of his, a vehicle so formidable that, until corrected, Jean had referred to as the truck.

Bam, Jean was in love again, so quick, so soon, she tried to warn her daughter that it was a mistake.

"How did it make you feel when Jean told you she was going to marry this man?" Henry asked.

"I was very angry," Mrs. Gareis said. She paused to glare at the defendant who continued to read prayers undaunted. "She was only twenty-one and we—my husband and I—felt this man was too old for her, that she was suffering an emotional rebound after Milton's death. We sent Jean to Boston but her separation from the man only made her fonder of him. When she returned home she was still determined to marry him. So we had the wedding in our home. That was August 16, 1945."

"Now tell us, Mrs. Gareis, what you know of your own knowledge of the married life of the Hetenyis."

"The newlyweds went to Pine Grove, California, where my son-in-law took a job as pastor at a Congregational Church."

"Your son-in-law is a Catholic priest, Mrs. Gareis?" Henry asked.

"He changes religions like a chameleon changes colors," Mrs. Gareis said.

There was light laughter. Judge O'Mara glared but didn't touch his gavel.

Henry asked if the witness had ever seen any indication of violence in her daughter's marriage.

Ms. Gareis said she had, one notable time in the spring of 1947. Her daughter and son-in-law were on their way to El Paso and Jean stopped to visit her parents.

"I noticed that my daughter had a bruised eye."

"Was this the first time you noticed bruises on Jean?"

"No. Twice before."

"Did you ask your daughter how she got the black eye?"

"I did not. I said to her that I did not want to talk about her husband behind his back but if a man strikes his wife it is no marriage."

Mrs. Gareis told a story of how in January 1948 she received a telephone call from her daughter: "Jean said she wanted me to come to El Paso and come to her aid. When I got there I found her with a bruised eye, cheek, and a missing tooth."

"Did you confront the defendant about your daughter's physical condition?"

"I certainly did. Diane, my granddaughter, was four-months old then and I told him this was no way for a father to act."

"What did he say to that?"

"He said for a woman to be a good wife she needed to have a beating once in a while."

There were three gasps from the gallery. They came in a

rhythmic sequence, followed by a fourth exclamation, more of a moan.

"And your daughter chose to stay with the defendant despite the physical violence?"

"Yes, she was a very religious woman and she wanted to stay married."

"No further questions," Henry said.

"No questions," Skivington chimed in.

The prosecution called a series of witnesses, church authorities and neighbors, who testified as to the defendant's brutality toward the deceased. One church official said that after the Hetenyis were called to Western New York the defendant had to be transferred from the pulpit and another time admonished because his behavior toward his wife was so brutal. Another witness said that after the Hetenyis had their second child, Jean sought advice concerning how to purchase and use contraceptives.

With the background established, the district attorney designed the next portion of his case to show the jury the movements, minute by minute, of the defendant and the victim on the day of the murder.

A man named Jack Strain took the stand and identified himself as the night deskman at Rochester's Sheraton Hotel. He testified that on the evening of April 22, Hetenyi entered the hotel lobby and asked him a series of odd questions, about the city of Rochester and the river that flows through it.

A witness named Robert Wright told the court that at 12:30 a.m. on the morning of April 23, he saw the defendant "lurking" on the Court Street Bridge. Wright testified that he accosted the defendant.

"I said, 'Hey, what are you doing there?'" Wright testified.

"And what did the defendant say to you?" Henry asked.

"He told me he was a visiting clergyman from out of town and interested in nature and rivers."

"Those were his exact words?"

"Yes, sir. He asked me where the river was deep and

where it was shallow. He asked about the currents, and he was particularly interested in if anything floating on the river was ever swept into the raceway that parallels the Genesee. He asked me where the raceway emptied and I told him I didn't know. I asked him his name and he said he'd rather not say. Just before he got back into his sedan he said that he was Chaplain Something-or-other, but I didn't catch the name."

The prosecution did a solid job placing Hetenyi in Rochester around midnight on the night before the body was found, and they showed that he was interested in the very river in which his wife was found floating.

They were on shakier ground when it came to demonstrating that Hetenyi had remained in Rochester until the evening of April 23, their sole witness being a waitress who identified the defendant as the man she had served spaghetti and a liquor drink to him around 11:00 p.m. Her identification was shakier than Henry would have liked, and under Skivington's cross-examination the waitress admitted that she wasn't one-hundred percent sure the man she saw was the defendant.

Three witnesses testified that Hetenyi was in a cleaning-up mood after his wife's murder. A pharmacist at an Amherst drug store said the defendant was in his store on Saturday, April 24, purchasing cleaning fluid.

Carl Baer, proprietor of Carl Baer's Garage, testified the defendant stopped in on the morning of April 24 and said he'd pay twice the normal fee for a thorough cleaning of his car.

Hetenyi's next stop apparently was at a Buffalo dry cleaner. Eli Konikoff, who worked there, said that the defendant came into the store that morning carrying a woman's gray coat.

"It looked like it had rust spots on it," Konikoff said of the coat.

"And what did the defendant want you to do with the

coat?" Henry asked.

"He wanted it dyed blue."

"The prosecution rests, your honor," Henry said. The prosecution's case had included forty-seven witnesses spread out over eight days.

"Very well, for scheduling purposes, how many witnesses do you plan on calling, Mr. Skivington?"

"None, your honor. It is the defense's stance that the prosecution's completely circumstantial case has failed to prove anything."

"You will be giving a summation of that stance?" Judge O'Mara asked.

"Yes, your honor."

"Are you prepared to do that now?"

"I am."

Court took a fifteen-minute bathroom break and when everyone was back in place and court was called to order, Skivington stood without notes to address the jury.

Jurors leaned forward a little bit before Skivington began to speak. The defense attorney had been railing against every prosecution move, every ruling by the judge, since day one, and he was clearly not happy with the way proceedings had gone.

"The holster should never have been allowed into evidence," Skivington said. "There is simply no way to connect it to the defendant."

The white-haired defense attorney told the jury that, truth be known, he wasn't sure why his client was on trial in the first place. The prosecution didn't know anything about this murder. They didn't even know where the murder happened. They didn't even know in which county the murder happened. Skivington wondered why the trial took place in Monroe County? It was ridiculous.

Skivington's argument became increasingly candid until some questioned the wisdom of his tact. He said the newspapers had been placing Hetenyi in the electric chair since he was arrested. There was no way that impartial jurors could be found in Monroe County, especially (and he blurted an uncomfortable truth) if *registered Democrats* were never allowed to serve.

Some of the jurors frowned at Skivington. Others looked slightly bewildered. Was he saying they were part of a conspiracy? Because, if so, they were pretty certain it wasn't true.

One thing, though: those jurors did not have wandering minds as the defense attorney spoke. They were riveted. The jury didn't necessarily like Skivington, but they appreciated the fact that he was never boring.

Skivington didn't disappoint. He characterized the case against his client as one clouded in "fog, mystery, and uncertainty."

He added, "Ladies and gentlemen of the jury, the prosecution has failed to provide a motive. Sure, the Hetenyis had some domestic difficulties. All couples do. There were other domestic situations that were far worse and more grievous than theirs. Tempers flare and men often strike wives they like and it does not end in dissolution of ties. The truth of the matter was that they loved one another. There is no other man in this case. There is no other woman. There is no insurance. There is no money profit. There is a complete absence of the things you usually find in a case where a man kills his wife. Let's look at my client's movements from the time his wife disappeared until his arrest. I think you will agree that they were not the actions of a guilty man..."

Last word went to the district attorney, who laughed at the defendant.

"Look at him," Henry said with a tone of disgust, "wearing clerical garments in court during the trial, a deliberate attempt to arouse your sympathy and prejudice, ladies and gentlemen of the jury."

"Objection, your honor," Skivington exclaimed. "This is the way the Reverend Hetenyi dresses for formal occasions."

"If he had any respect for his church, he would not dress that way in court while on trial for murder. He's a fraud. The church to him is a selfish proposition to get out of it only what he can," Henry said.

"Gentlemen..." the judge said with a scowl.

Before O'Mara could rule, Henry withdrew the statement. What the heck? It could be stricken from the record but the jury couldn't unhear it.

Henry got down to brass tacks and counted off for the jury the evidence against Hetenyi. Jean was killed with two .25 gunshot wounds to the chest. Blood was found in Hetenyi's '47 Olds. In that same car a .25 bullet was found inside a door. The door bullets and the victim bullets were fired from the same gun. Hetenyi wanted a Buffalo dry cleaner to clean blood from inside his car. Hetenyi beat his wife. Early Saturday morning, April 23, several witnesses saw Hetenyi in the Rochester area being inquisitive regarding the flow of the Genesee River. A witness found a holster capable of holding a .25 near the spot where the body was found in the river. Witnesses had seen a holster of similar description in Hetenyi's possession.

Judge O'Mara charged the jury. He took the wind out of Skivington's "the prosecution doesn't know where the murder took place" argument.

The judge said, "It makes no difference as to where those shots were fired in view of the evidence that has been presented during the course of this trial." Judge O'Mara added that, as the body was found in Monroe County, that was sufficient to "create a presumption that the shots were fired here, too."

Skivington had requested that the judge instruct the jury that determining that the murder took place in Monroe County was a prerequisite to finding the defendant guilty.

Judge O'Mara refused.

It was about five o'clock on the afternoon of December 15, 1949 when the jurors were sent to their deliberation room to determine Hetenyi's fate. They deliberated for five hours without reaching a verdict and decided to call it a night.

The ten men and two women were taken to rooms in the nearby Powers Hotel to spend the night. They started up again first thing the next morning and rapidly reached a decision. It was about nine o'clock in the morning of December 16 when a bailiff informed Judge O'Mara. Two and a half hours later everyone was again assembled in the courtroom for the reading of the verdict.

Throughout the trial Hetenyi had appeared distracted (by prayer) but calm. When he came into court for the reading of the verdict, he was visibly nervous, even unkempt. He seemed a little wild around the eyes as if he had not slept.

"All rise," a bailiff said. Skivington stood close by Hetenyi's side and placed a comforting hand on his shoulder.

"Ladies and gentlemen of the jury, have you reached a verdict?" Judge O'Mara asked.

"We have, your honor. We find the defendant guilty of murder in the second degree."

Hetenyi shivered a moment but otherwise gave no outward signs of emotion. He was quickly led away.

"We will of course appeal," Skivington told a battery of reporters out in the hall.

On January 16, 1950, Judge O'Mara sentenced Hetenyi to fifty years to life in prison.

"I'm leaving everything to God," Hetenyi said.

The appeal was argued on May 15, 1950 before the Appellate Division, Fourth Department. Skivington appealed the conviction on two grounds: 1) The prosecution introduced into evidence the holster found near where the body was discovered but never demonstrated that it belonged to the defendant. 2) The murder trial had taken place in Monroe County, but there was no evidence that the murder took place in Monroe County.

The appellate panel said it was an error to refuse to charge the defendant's request that the jury be required to find that the murder took place in Monroe County, and that it was reversible error when the judge told the jury it made no difference where those shots were fired. The court also concluded that there was no evidence connecting the holster to the defendant—that he'd been seen with one that looked like it wasn't enough—and allowing the holster into evidence was also reversible error. The appellate court determined that Hetenyi's conviction was dismissed and a new trial was ordered.

After sixteen months in prison, Hetenyi was granted a second trial. The re-trial, for the D.A., represented a lot of work he didn't think was necessary. Did anyone think Hetenyi *didn't* kill his wife? But there was one facet of the appellate decision that he liked: Because of the decision's specific nature, he now knew where his prosecution needed to be bolstered. He needed to present evidence that Hetenyi wore that holster.

As for the location of the crime, he didn't see the decision's point at all. Physical evidence indicated the murder had taken place in Hetenyi's car. It didn't matter where the car was when the murder took place. County Judge James P. O'Connor, who presided over the second trial, agreed up to a point.

The new trial began on April 25, 1951. Once again Skivington wailed for more diversity on the jury and the new jury had more of a middle- and lower-middle-class feel to it. At least some registered Democrats had been included in the jury pool.

The prosecution's case was nearly identical in thrust to the one previously presented, but far more detailed. Along with

Les McMahon, Clara Beach, the authorities who worked the case, and the witnesses who saw Hetenyi acting suspiciously around the time of the murder, there were also three new witnesses, one who came all the way from California to help connect the defendant to the missing murder weapon. The prosecution put witnesses on the stand for longer than two weeks.

In his closing statement, Henry said, "I say to you that lonely dark place on the bank of the Genesee River is the place at which you must infer in light of all the evidence in this case that this crime took place. By what ruse did this defendant bring her down there, you'll never know, and I'll never know, not as long as he stands on his Constitutional rights so-called."

"Objection!" Skivington cried.

"Overruled," Judge O'Conner said.

"What kind of a man is Hetenyi? People cut him slack because he is a man of the cloth. Is he? He's an imposter, a fraud, and no more a man of the cloth than I am. Ask him how many times he has changed religions. He can't tell you. He can't count them all."

When charging the jury, Judge O'Conner said, "You will recall, ladies and gentlemen, that during the course of this trial a great deal has been said about where this killing occurred, that is, the venue or locus of the crime. Under this indictment, this defendant cannot be convicted of the crime charged or of any of the degrees of homicide unless you find this killing took place in Monroe County. This is a question of fact that must be determined by the jury. However, the standard of proof that is required under our law by which you are to determine this fact is distinctly different from the standard of proof required in determining the fact that the defendant did the killing. The distinction, ladies and gentlemen, is of great importance. You must find that the defendant killed the deceased beyond a reasonable doubt…However, the venue of the crime is not a part of the crime itself and need not be proven beyond a reasonable doubt. In the absence of direct proof as to the venue, or the place where the killing occurred, that question may be determined by circumstantial evidence from all relevant evidence.

"In this case there appears to be no direct evidence as to where the shooting actually took place, so you must rely upon circumstantial evidence in determining that fact; and again, you are permitted to draw inferences from all the facts and circumstances in the case…

"The proof is sufficient if, from all the facts and circumstances introduced in evidence, venue may be fairly and reasonably inferred. If, from the facts in evidence, the only rational conclusion that can be drawn is that the crime was committed in this county as alleged the proof is sufficient."

Skivington's gamble did not pay off. After five and a half hours of deliberation, the second jury too brought back a guilty verdict, but this time to first-degree murder.

At a later hearing Judge O'Connor sentenced Hetenyi to death, to be executed in the electric chair.

There was no hurry in executing Hetenyi. As with all murder-one convictions, the case was automatically reviewed by the Court of Appeals. If the conviction was upheld the case would be sent to the governor for possible but unlikely clemency.

On April 23, 1952, the Court of Appeals threw out Hetenyi's second conviction by a four-to-three count. The panel decided that Henry had committed a reversible error during his closing statement when he made references to the defendant's character ("he's a fraud"), and standing on his "constitutional rights so-called."

A third trial was ordered.

George Skivington said he was done. He'd defended Hetenyi twice, and it was time for him to move on to other things. Hetenyi subsequently announced that he had retained lawyer William L. "Bill" Clay to defend him.

Clay's first order of business was to get the third trial out of Monroe County, where at that point a fair jury could not be found. Justice John VanVoorhis granted the change of venue.

The third trial began on January 19, 1952, in Supreme Court, Onondaga County, Syracuse, New York, with Justice Earl Barstow of Utica presiding. There was much repetition, of course. Les's dad drove him there. Clara Beach made the trip. The news from the third trial came after Henry presented the prosecution's case. Bill Clay decided to put on a case on behalf of his client and called as his first witness Hetenyi's aged mother, who told the jury she believed the shooting took place in Erie County, that her daughter-in-law had committed suicide in their Amherst garage.

"Where was your son when the shooting occurred?" Clay asked.

"He was in the bathroom."

"He heard the shots?"

"Yes."

"How do you know?"

"Because he came running out of the bathroom and into the garage. He put Jean in the car and drove to the hospital," the seventy-eight year old woman said in her thick Hungarian accent.

"Did you ever see your daughter-in-law again?"

"I did not."

"Did you ask your son later about what had happened?"

"I didn't."

Henry took a look at the jury, saw they weren't even close to buying it, and declined to cross-examine. He didn't even mention it in his summary. Mrs. Hetenyi's bald-faced lies were damning in their own way.

The Onondaga County jury found Hetenyi guilty of murder in the second degree, which got Hetenyi off of death row. At the sentencing hearing he was sent back to prison for forty years.

After the third conviction, Hetenyi's time in the New York State correctional system was split between Attica and the Clinton Correctional Facility in Dannemora. He used every minute to scheme a way to earn his release. He filed writs of *habeas corpus* and appeals in longhand and submitted them to the courts.

In July 1965 a U.S. Circuit Court of Appeals in New York ruled that Hetenyi could not be convicted of first-degree murder in a subsequent trial if he was convicted of second degree for the same offense at an earlier trial. In other words, the prosecution could not use a mistrial as an excuse to "up the ante" on a defendant, in essence punishing him for making the people prosecute him a second time. The ruling stated that, yes, Hetenyi could have a new trial involving the murder of his wife, but he had to face only the second-degree murder charges that he had been convicted of the first time.

Hetenyi's appeal counsel, the court-appointed Ernest J. Brown, a law professor at Harvard, argued that Hetenyi being subjected to a new trial was placing him in double jeopardy in violation of his constitutional rights by being tried twice for first-degree murder after the jury at his first trial reduced his charge to second-degree.

The judge's decision that called for Hetenyi to endure a fourth murder trail was sent to the U.S. Supreme Court, which in February 1966, refused to review it. That meant that any fourth trial was bound to be a legal quagmire. Hetenyi was again unable to get himself a lawyer. Bill Clay sent his regrets, saying he had too many legal and trial commitments to take on Hetenyi again.

Erie County Court Judge Frederick M. Marshall spoke with sixty-nine-year-old criminal defense lawyer Sidney Z. Davidson and asked if he'd be willing to take the job should a fourth Hetenyi trial occur. Davidson, a veteran of two-hundred homicide cases as a defense lawyer who had just completed a stint as a City Court judge, said he would. Davidson's assistant was expected to be Barry R. Hill, a young and energetic Syracuse lawyer who could spell the aging Davidson.

Judge Marshall signed an order to have the defendant transferred from his Attica cell to a comfier home in the Onondaga County Public Safety Building.

But on April 20, 1966, when Hetenyi appeared in a Syracuse courtroom before Judge Marshall, Hetenyi was without counsel. He would be presenting his own argument, he announced, and that argument was that New York State no longer had a right to prosecute him. Hetenyi argued his point well, at one point moving to dismiss the original indictment against him on the grounds that it was "tainted" and based in part on "perjured testimony."

Hetenyi argued, "The state cannot be permitted to try and retry this charge until the defendant is dead in prison of old age."

On May 3, Hetenyi was arraigned on fresh murder-two charges before Judge Marshall, now with court-appointed defense attorney Alexander Hercsa of Syracuse at his side, but a fourth Hetenyi trial was averted when Hetenyi pleaded guilty to a reduced charge of first-degree manslaughter. By doing so, he rendered himself immediately eligible for parole. The district attorney offered the reduced charge and Hetenyi grabbed at it.

Onondaga County D.A. John C. Little found the move appealing because he was catching flack for the cost of a fourth trial. Getting a conviction out of a jury became more difficult as time passed. Witnesses died. Those who survived had faded memories. The third trial had cost the taxpayers $18,000. The fourth trial figured to be more expensive yet.

At his June 1, 1966 sentencing hearing, held in the ancient Onondaga County courthouse, Hetenyi entered with a smile, which was different. He waved at the D.A., who frowned at him. He waved at Sheriff Skinner, who waved back.

At the hearing, Hetenyi made an impassioned plea for

mercy to Judge Marshall. Hetenyi said his only ambition at this point in his life was to join a monastery. He would live a life of penance as a Roman Catholic monk.

Hetenyi sat nervously, drumming his fingers on the defense table in front of him as his attorney Alexander Hercsa said it was a case that had gone on for too long. It was time for everyone involved to "wash the case out of their hair. I think it's time we write a finish to it. George Hetenyi plans to enter the religious life where he will hopefully do penance for anything he might have done in the past. He has suffered every single minute of the past seventeen-odd years and there is no question in my mind that he is probably going to suffer with himself for what he has done. Society to some extent may owe Hetenyi a debt. He has caused federal courts to set aside statutes of the State of New York which stood on the books for a number of years and forced a defendant to play a game of Russian Roulette."

Judge Marshall cited a series of recent higher court decisions that would have made convicting Hetenyi at any subsequent trial next to impossible, and agreed with District Attorney Little that allowing the defrocked clergyman to plead guilty to the lesser charge had been the correct move.

The judge sentenced Hetenyi to "not less than one year and the maximum of which shall terminate on the sixth day of June 1966."

Hetenyi smiled from ear to ear. He'd been sentenced to time served, plus six days. Seventeen years had passed since his wife's death. After hearing his sentence, he was taken by elevator into the courthouse basement, where he and his guard were met by a turnkey that took them through a secret security tunnel to the Onondaga County jail.

"The van isn't available to us until tomorrow morning," the turnkey said.

"I get to spend the night here?"

"You're our guest for the night."

"Better than Attica," Hetenyi said with a big smile.

Sheriff Skinner wanted to talk to Hetenyi's lawyer.

"Hercsa, do me a favor. Ask him where he threw the gun."

"Sorry, Sheriff. I don't want to embarrass him with the question."

In the morning they put Hetenyi in a state van for transport back to Attica. While standing in the basement awaiting the turnkey, Hetenyi was overheard saying, "It's over."

His attention then turned to practical matters. He'd had a public defender in Onondaga County who'd dropped out. The guy took the "big book" with him, a bound copy of transcripts and documents pertaining to Hetenyi's first trial, and he wanted to get it back.

According to his lawyers, hitting the monastery wasn't Hetenyi's first stop. Hetenyi's mom had passed away since his last trial when she testified on his behalf, and he planned to visit her grave in Ogdensburg, then visit relatives in New York City, and then start his monastic existence.

The news that Hetenyi was going to be released to walk in public again horrified John C. Little. The D.A. moved that there be a court inquiry to establish Hetenyi used a pistol in the murder of his wife and thus subject to another ten years in prison. Judge Marshall denied the motion.

On June 6, 1966 (6/6/66), while future serial killer Arthur Shawcross celebrated his twenty-first birthday, and Kathy Bernhard and George-Ann Formicola lived out the last weeks of their lives attending Wheatland-Chili High School in Scottsville, George Hetenyi was released from Attica prison a free man.

On his way out a reporter asked him which monastery he was going to enter. Hetenyi said, "No comment."

There were reports that Hetenyi had been getting mail from a Midwestern monastery welcoming him as soon as he was freed from prison.

Hercsa had done a great job for Hetenyi, got him on the

outside with a clean slate. But he did like to hear himself talk and when asked a question he had a tendency to answer it.

"Is Hetenyi on good enough terms with the Catholic Church to get into a monastery?" a reporter asked.

"He was excommunicated by the Roman Catholic Church after his first conviction, but the excommunication was lifted in 1954—so he's clear to become a monk if he so wishes," Hercsa said.

"Will Hetenyi be seeing his two children?"

"No, that's a part of his life that everyone is forgetting about."

Those kids were almost adults by this time. They'd gone to live with their grandmother in California and never came back.

With a bus ticket purchased by Warden Vincent R. Mancusi in his pocket, Hetenyi was picked up by the Department of Corrections van along with two other prisoners being released. Also in his pocket was half the pay he had earned in prison clerical jobs. He was taken to the Trailways bus station in Batavia on Court Street and dropped off at 9:50 a.m.

Hetenyi got out of the van and was accosted by reporters.

"It's over," he repeated. "Please leave me alone."

He turned and walked into the bus terminal. The reporters followed. They wanted to know where he was headed.

"Now get away from me, leave me alone, I told you," Hetenyi said, sounding irritated.

The interaction between the newspapermen and the ex-con was different enough to draw a crowd of curiosity-seekers. Hetenyi pointed at several females who'd stopped to watch the action.

"These ladies have civil rights too you know," he said, but no one understood what that meant.

Hetenyi could see that there was no way he was going to be unobserved so he went about his business. He had a quiet conversation with a man he appeared to have met by chance, and then went to a ticket window and cashed in his unused ticket. He had been carrying three packages but he left one in the depot and left with the man, now carrying just two packages.

Hetenyi got into the man's car and they drove, with reporters following, down Main Street, Batavia. One scribe took down the license plate number and discovered it belonged to a sixty-two-year-old Batavia man named Fred S. Baker, a retired correction officer who worked at Attica during Hetenyi's time there.

The pair went shopping. Hetenyi bought a new hat and asked the clerk to throw out his old one. He bought some luggage. He also went into a jewelers and a men's clothes store, where he made unspecified purchases. From there they went to a restaurant on Main Street where Hetenyi ordered a steak and left the waitress a seventy-five-cent tip.

George Hetenyi did not become a monk. In fact, he remarried, marrying Maria Hendrika. He died in April 1977 at age 67. He'd been living in Phoenix, Arizona, and was buried there.

Before shutting the book on the Hetenyi case, I once again considered what Ol' Lady Tyler had said to my mom about somebody dumping Jean Hetenyi into Black Creek near Stallman Drive and the Genesee Junction.

Could a body dumped in the water there end up at the spot where it was found, on the east shore of the Genesee up by Delaware Avenue?

One thing I had to take into consideration was that the creek in 1949 had its mouth just south of the railroad trestle. Years later, a huge engineering job dug a big ditch and channeled Black Creek's water further south, closer to the Ballantyne Bridge, to help alleviate spring flooding.

So, in 1949, a body floating in Black Creek would enter the

Genesee closer to where the body was found, only about three-hundred yards upstream, than it would if the same method of disposal were attempted today.

Time was another consideration. How long would it take for a body dumped in the creek near Genesee Junction to get to Delaware Avenue? And wasn't there a far greater chance that the body would get snagged somewhere along the creek than after it entered the stronger current of the river?

I had seen aerial photos of Black Creek flowing into the Genesee and you could see the dark silt of the creek pushing fully half-way across the river. Would a body entering the Genesee on the west side get caught on a snag on the east bank? Hard to say, but perhaps feasible.

As for Ol' Lady Tyler's theory regarding Jean Hetenyi's true killer, I'm pretty sure she had it wrong.

Black Creek

Sister Maureen

THE BABY IN THE CONVENT

During the 1970s, Our Lady of Lourdes convent on Warrington Drive in Brighton was part of the Congregation of the Sisters of St. Joseph. It was a quiet place, its residents mostly teachers at local parochial schools, and the very last place you'd expect to become a crime scene. But on Tuesday, April 27, 1976, that is exactly what happened.

That was the day that thirty-five-year-old Sister Maureen Murphy—the former Carol A. Murphy, a eighteen-year veteran of the convent, and the director of and pre-school teacher at the Trinity Montessori School on French Road in Pittsford—was found bleeding heavily from the vagina in her room by her neighbor nuns.

One nun called an ambulance and the bleeding Sister Maureen was rushed to Genesee Hospital.

Sister Maureen was a tiny woman: four-eleven, normally less than one-hundred pounds. Doctors quickly determined that Sister Maureen had just given birth. This was news to her neighboring nuns who had no idea that she was pregnant, and certainly had no clue as to how she got that way.

Bizarrely, instead of notifying police or an ambulance, the doctors told the nuns accompanying Sister Maureen to go back to the convent and search for the baby.

Those nuns did as they'd been told and quickly made a horrifying discovery. They found a lifeless male infant in a plastic wastebasket that had been placed behind a bookcase and out of view in Sister Maureen's room.

The baby had a cloth stuffed in its mouth. A blue woman's nightgown was tied around its neck. The nuns removed the baby from the wastebasket, wrapped it in a blanket and took it to Genesee Hospital where it was pronounced dead at 8:05 p.m.

The ambulance attendants who had transported Sister Maureen from the convent to the hospital were asked if they'd seen anything suspicious while picking up the woman. They said they made a cursory examination of the area but nothing thorough. Their concentration was on the bleeding woman and it didn't occur to them immediately that she'd just given birth. You know, she was a nun and all.

The county morgue was notified twenty-five minutes later. Monroe County Medical Examiner Dr. John Edland assigned his assistant Dr. George Abbott the sad task of performing a post-mortem procedure on the infant. The autopsy was mandatory because it was a suspicious death.

After the autopsy, Dr. Edland announced the results, saying the child weighed six pounds, twelve ounces, and had been born alive. He could tell that this had not been a stillbirth by the traces of oxygen in the infant's lungs and intestinal tract. The child had lived, if only for a matter of minutes.

The medical examiner ruled the death a homicide: asphyxiation by gagging.

The men in charge of the investigation would be Brighton Police Chief Eugene Shaw and Monroe County District Attorney Lawrence Kurlander.

Shaw told the press that he didn't think grand jury hearings were necessary as an arrest would be made and a suspect would be formally charged before any grand jury action could be taken.

The papers did not initially report that, in addition to the tiny body, a nun had been found bleeding—but this statement by the D.A. indicated to a careful reader that the child's mother was known and she was the *only suspect* in the death of the baby.

Of course, because the baby was found in a convent, reporters were chomping at the bit for details, so officials had to say "no comment" again and again. There would be no immediate details regarding how the baby was found or who were its parents.

Despite the silence from authorities, reporters had their ways of acquiring information and quickly learned that a bleeding nun had been taken to the hospital. It wasn't hard to put two and two together. Any doubts that the nun had been the mother were destroyed when a medical source told a reporter that the nun had delivered the afterbirth—that is, the placenta and fetal membranes—in the hospital.

Just when the situation couldn't get any freakier, doctors told Sister Maureen that she had had a baby and was in the hospital, and she looked at them like they had two heads.

"What baby? I wasn't pregnant," she said. "That's ridiculous. I'm a virgin."

A canvass of the convent found not a single nun who said she knew Sister Maureen was pregnant. How was that possible? Were the nuns unusually unobservant, or were they liars?

Pregnancy, in just about every case, is a very difficult thing to mask. That would seem to be especially true for a diminutive woman. Some thought those nuns had to know. The only other possibility was that a nun being pregnant was so unthinkable that they couldn't think it.

"When did you know something was wrong with Sister

Maureen?" police asked the nuns.

The consensus said the first indication was when Sister Maureen called in sick on the morning she gave birth. She had complained of a tummy ache, but had worked the day before. She said she hoped to feel better by lunchtime and might make it to work for the afternoon school session.

At the hospital, Sister Maureen was listed in "satisfactory" condition. Of biggest concern to the doctors were the indications she demonstrated of mental-health issues. (Maybe the entire convent should have its collective head examined, some thought.)

Sister M. Jeamesine Riley, superior general of the order, handed out a written statement to the effect that they were "cooperating fully" with the police investigation. The statement was as cool as the other side of the pillow. You could feel thin lips clamping shut.

Reporters contacted as many of Sister Maureen's high school friends as they could find and were told that she was a sweet and lovely woman, a "perfect lady." Those friends could not imagine that the stories they were hearing were true. The Carol they knew from school could never do such a thing.

Those same reporters had far less luck getting anyone who'd known Sister Maureen in the last eighteen years to talk. Both at the convent and the school where Sister Maureen taught, nobody had anything to say.

"Sorry," one nun admitted, "the superiors of the order have asked us not to comment."

By the following day, the nun in question had been booked on charges of second-degree murder and everyone knew the name Sister Maureen Murphy.

At the convent, Sister M. Jeamesine Riley contacted the diocese and received permission to retain a defense attorney for Sister Maureen. The permission was granted and attorney

Charles Crimi was brought in to represent the nun.

Law enforcement in Monroe County was starting to feel a little shell-shocked. There had been a number of bizarre and disturbing crimes committed in the recent past, and the dead baby in the convent seemed like a further step into the twilight zone of crime.

Only sixteen days before Sister Maureen had her son, seven-year-old Michelle McMurray was found dead outside her apartment building on Rochester's Jay Street. She'd been left alone by her young mother as mom went to a corner bar, bought a pack of cigarettes, and picked up a man to bring back with her. The case was troubling on its own, made more so by the little girl's initials. It had been three years since the last "Double-Initial Murder" in Rochester, and there was terror that the creep who killed Carmen Colon, Wanda Walkowicz, and Michelle Maenza was back.[1] Police soothed the masses, saying they were pretty sure this was a separate deal.

(The Michelle McMurray case stayed closed for years until DNA technology was in place. The building's creepy superintendent threw away a cigarette butt that was confiscated by police. The butt had spit on it from which a DNA profile was developed, a profile that matched DNA evidence found on little Michelle.)

There was also a serial rapist on the loose. Since late March, three girls aged ten through seventeen were raped in Rochester's 19th ward, along with two more college girls on the campus of the University of Rochester. The campus rapist held his victims at knifepoint.

Now, a baby in a convent. What next?

A search was on for the father of Sister Maureen's baby.

---

[1] See *Nightmare in Rochester: The Double-Initial Murders* by Michael Benson and Donald A. Tubman, Brooklyn, N.Y.: Benson Books, 2018.

An investigation into her recent past revealed that nine months before giving birth she had gone to Connecticut. She was on vacation there and stayed at her sister's summerhouse. Word was she met a man. Two men from the district attorney's office and a cop from the Brighton Police went to Connecticut to see what they could learn. The man was located and admitted to the affair. He said he had no idea that Sister Maureen was a nun, didn't know she'd become pregnant, and appreciated it if his name could be kept out of it, which it was.

Sister Maureen's sister, who owned the summerhouse, was Susan McCormick of Concord, New Hampshire. Initial attempts to contact McCormack were unsuccessful. Then they learned that McCormack was visiting her mother in Florida.

Police learned that Carol Murphy had been born in the city of Rochester in 1939. Her dad, Paul J. Murphy, died in 1975. When Sister Maureen's Genesee Hospital doctors learned that she'd suffered the loss of a parent in the recent past, they wondered if this trauma might have triggered whatever issues Sister Maureen was now having.

Her mom Helen lived in Florida, and she had two brothers in addition to her sister Susan. Sister Maureen was a graduate of Nazareth Academy, class of 1957, on Lake Avenue in the city. She was class secretary her freshman year, and vice-president as a junior. She was on the yearbook staff, dramatics club, the French Club, and the mission crusade.

Her family lived on Frost Avenue on Rochester's west side and they regularly attended the Immaculate Conception Church on South Plymouth Avenue.

The Sisters of St. Joseph ran Nazareth Academy, so it was an easy transition to go from Nazareth to the convent, which is what Carol did, taking Maureen as her nun name.

In addition to becoming a nun, Sister Maureen attended Nazareth College and earned in 1965 a bachelor of science degree in history, and subsequently a master's degree in education.

Since the autumn of 1975 she had been the administrator at Trinity Montessori School in Pittsford. She was considered an expert in pre-school education and was often consulted for advice from other parochial schools in the diocese. On May 1, 1976, Sister Maureen was booked in her hospital room on suspicion of murder.

That same day, Sister Maureen's brother Richard Murphy contacted Dr. Edland at the morgue and said he would take custody of the body and make funeral arrangements. At that point, the little body was still in a drawer at the county morgue, a tag around its tiny toe. The Congregation of the Sisters of St. Joseph promised that they would pay all funeral bills.

Dr. Edland told a reporter from the morning paper that it was his understanding the baby would be cremated. The actual arrangements were to be kept private. The medical examiner characterized the case as "the most unusual and upsetting" that he'd ever been associated with.

On May 2, a member of the Catholic diocese broke the wall of silence. He was the Right Rev. Monsignor Leslie Whalen. He told a reporter that the whole Our Lady of Lourdes convent was struggling with what happened. It would be a hard thing to accept in any circumstances, but in a community where one thing everyone had in common was a pledge of celibacy, it was particularly mind-boggling.

The nuns had had to come to grips with a number of uncomfortable truths. Sister Maureen had sex with someone. She became pregnant and kept that pregnancy a secret. She kept the secret very well and no one knew of it until it was too late. She gave birth right there in the convent. She apparently freaked out and killed the child, perhaps stuffing its mouth initially to keep it quiet.

It was too much. How could such a thing happen? The nuns of the convent were walking around in a daze.

Monsignor Whalen said, "We realize no one is perfect. There has been an outpouring of sympathy and concern, mostly by word of mouth. There has been a deep feeling of sadness. It has all made us aware that everyone is human. Today, the responses to liturgical readings during the mass at the church seemed quietly sad."

He added that masses with the nuns are usually quieter than normal and because he didn't like to sing they often celebrated the mass without any music.

"We find forgiveness when we turn to God. As an example of our forgiveness we forgive those we find it difficult to forgive. In the midst of our sorrow this past week, we thank God for the good things that He has given us. We praise the Lord. In Jesus' name, we preach penance for the forgiveness of sin."

Other members of the congregation, not held back by the wall of silence, were surprisingly sympathetic to the tiny nun.

"She must have been very distressed," said one woman.

"She was the sweetest, cutest little thing," another said. "We are all so very sorry about this."

A third added, "Our hearts are bleeding. All week long there were police cars, reporters' cars, people asking questions. It's been a rough week for us."

And she *was* the sweetest, cutest thing. Even knowing about her what they knew, folks struggled with the reality of what had occurred. Almost no one considered the possibility, the very real possibility, that she was a monster.

Physically, Sister Maureen recovered quickly from her childbirth, and was transferred to Monroe Community Hospital where her remaining mental problems could better be dealt with.

On May 6, Sister Maureen was arraigned in her new hospital. Monroe County Court Judge Hyman T. Maas presided over the arraignment, which took about fifteen minutes, and was held in the hospital's mental-health ward conference room.

Also in attendance at the arraignment were Charles Crimi and Anthony Palermo, Sister Maureen's defense team, and Assistant District Attorney Joseph Valentino, who would prosecute her case.

Judge Haas read Sister Maureen her rights and questioned her to make sure she understood them.

"Yes, I understand," she said in a tiny voice.

Judge Maas set bail at $5,000. That was posted immediately, although Sister Maureen did not leave the hospital. She said she wanted to go home to the convent but her doctors said she had to stay where she was for the time being. She was alone in a room, and a Brighton Police guard stood in the hallway to make sure she didn't wander off.

Sister Maureen did not plead at the arraignment. A grand jury was scheduled to hear testimony in her case and if they brought down a new arraignment she would be asked to plead at that time.

Judge Maas scheduled a preliminary hearing in the matter of People v. Sister Maureen, for May 17, but it was delayed until June because ADA Valentino fell in his home and broke his elbow.

Around that time, Sister Maureen was discharged from Community Hospital. She was taken to a room in a convent, but not Our Lady of Lourdes, where returning to her room would have meant returning to the scene of the alleged crime, perhaps too much for her fragile psyche to take.

So when she got to go home she didn't go home at all. Her location was supposed to remain undisclosed, and it was, but some reporters knew where she was because they'd followed her, following her wherever she went.

Her lawyers said that she was "still under medical care," but offered no details.

As Valentino's shattered elbow slowly healed, the Monroe County Grand Jury heard witnesses in the case. On May 24, attorney Palermo caused a stir, announcing that Sister

Maureen would be testifying at the hearing.

He said the decision to have her testify was "in the interests of full disclosure of all the facts." Palermo added that the defense also planned on calling a pair of psychiatrists to testify.

The District Attorney's Office announced that they would be calling a psychiatrist to testify in the Sister Maureen case as well. He was Dr. Robert Stubblefield, a clinical professor in Yale University's psychiatry department, and one of fifteen witnesses the prosecution planned to call.

Later that day, Dr. Stubblefield visited Sister Maureen and interviewed her for two hours. He then went immediately to the grand jury and testified as to what he had learned.

On May 26, Sister Maureen testified before the grand jury for two hours. Since grand jury hearings are secret, it was not disclosed what she said. What we do know is that she appeared pale but composed when she entered in the company of District Attorney Lawrence Kurlander, his assistants Howard Relin and Joseph Valentino, arm in a sling.

The grand jury heard testimony through the first week in June. They had five choices: first-degree murder, second-degree murder, first-degree manslaughter, second-degree manslaughter, or criminally negligent homicide. Actually six. They could have chosen not to indict her at all.

The jurors decided to indict Sister Maureen on a charge of first-degree manslaughter, which was a step down from the second-degree murder charge she'd been facing before. The grand jury explained that the lesser charge was chosen because they believed Sister Maureen was "extremely emotionally disturbed" when she killed the child.

Defense attorney Palermo was asked about his strategy. He would not commit to putting on an insanity defense, but he did say that Sister Maureen "lost consciousness and awareness" during the birth of her baby.

Sister Maureen was arraigned for the lesser manslaughter charge, negating the earlier murder two charge. This time the judge did not go to her; she went to the judge at the Monroe County courthouse downtown.

She was asked her plea.

"Not guilty," she said in a whispery voice.

For her court appearance, Sister Maureen wore a white dress. She wore sunglasses as she entered and exited the courthouse.

Sister Maureen enters court.

After the new arraignment hearing, Palermo issued a press release that read: "This case will now proceed to a trial on the merits. At the trial, the prosecution will be required to establish each and every element of the alleged crime by proof beyond a reasonable doubt. The indictment charges that Sister Maureen acted with specific intent to cause the death of an infant. This is emphatically denied. Incident and prior to the delivery of the infant, Sister Maureen sustained a massive severe loss of blood, resulting in a loss of consciousness and awareness. This will be established by medical and psychiatric proof, which confirms that Sister Maureen never possessed any intent to harm or injure the infant.

"It is appropriate at this time to dispel some of the misstatements in the media, as well as rumors, suspicions and conjecture relating to the conception involved in this matter. All of the facts surrounding this enormous tragedy will be disclosed at the trial.

"The uncontroverted evidence will show that no present or past member of any religious community was involved in the conception. In addition, the evidence will show that Sister Maureen never met or communicated with the individual prior or subsequent to the incident, which occurred in August 1975. The facts will further demonstrate that the event was not the result of any romantic relationship.

"Since the tragedy has unfolded, Sister Maureen has received hundreds upon hundreds of letters from all over the world, extending compassion, understanding, and support.

"On behalf of Sister Maureen, her co-counsel Charles F. Crimi and Anthony R. Palermo express sincere appreciation to all for the comfort these messages have brought."

When Kurlander read Palermo's press release he was quick to point out that the prosecution disagreed on a number of points. For one thing, he objected to the passage that stated that Sister Maureen had not had a "romantic relationship" with the child's father. Kurlander thought this implied that Sister Maureen had been raped, which was not the case.

A reporter asked, "Any word from Connecticut and the search for the father?"

"No comment," Kurlander said.

A lot had gone on, the wheels of justice were grinding away, but one thing remained unchanged. Five weeks had passed since the infant died and its body remained in the

Monroe County Morgue. Dr. Edland was getting frustrated.

"Just out of simple human decency, I want to see the baby have a proper burial," the medical examiner said. The child was never given a name. His I.D. read "Baby Boy Murphy".

Dr. Edland was asked if anyone had come forward to claim the body, and he refused to elaborate.

"I can't say anything about it, okay?" he said.

"Have you reached out to find someone who'll claim the body?" a reporter inquired.

"Yes. I have reached out to members of Sister Maureen's family and to the Roman Catholic diocese."

He then implied that the hold up wasn't that the baby was abandoned, but that it was evidence.

"It has been suggested that the defense might want a second autopsy by their own surgeon," the medical examiner said. "But the time has just about passed for that."

"How is the body being preserved?"

"The body is frozen—has been since early May, hopefully reducing decomposition."

He added that there was no reason to think his own autopsy was inadequate in any way, and emphasized that his methodology and results would all be available as evidence at Sister Maureen's trial.

On June 18, Sister Maureen's legal team filed a "notice of defense" with the Monroe County Clerk's Office. The notice stated that their case "intends to rely upon the defense of mental disease or defect." The notice was required in cases in which the defendant's "state of mind" was a consideration in their defense.

Palermo took questions from reporters regarding the notice, moments after it was filed.

"Does this mean that Sister Maureen is not going to contest that she killed the baby?"

"Not at all," Palermo said. "Every issue in the case will be open and the prosecution will have the burden of proving each point beyond a reasonable doubt. This notice just puts the prosecution on notice that this will be an issue in the case. The notice relates to the whole state of mind at the time of the offense. We still emphatically deny that she ever intended to kill the infant."

Palermo then distributed Xerox copies of the notice, to make sure the papers and TV got it right.

The notice read: "Please take notice that the defendant intends to relay upon the defense of mental disease or defect pursuant to Section 30.05 of the Penal Law, then to offer proof of such defense at the trial of this action."

The referenced law read, "A person is not criminally responsible for conduct if at the time of such conduct, as a result of mental disease or defect, he lacks substantial capacity to know or appreciate either the nature and consequence of such conduct, or that such conduct was wrong."

The summer came and went. Lawyers on both sides put their ducks in order. At the beginning of September Valentino said the defense would be ready in about two-and-a-half months, or the middle of November.

Both Valentino and Crimi for the defense had filed a series of pre-trial motions. In those days before the current discovery rules, Crimi asked for permission to view some prosecution materials in the case. Judge Hyman did not immediately rule, but instead reviewed a transcript of the pertinent grand jury testimony. He then granted the defense an opportunity to get a limited upfront view of the prosecution's case.

The evidence the defense received permission to see consisted of the materials seized by investigators from Sister Maureen's room and a transcript of the grand jury testimony from the prosecution's three psychiatrists.

When the middle of November arrived, both sides were still weeks away from being ready. December at the earliest was the word. Then the process of getting the case to trial was further complicated by the January issue of *True Story* magazine, which contained an article about Sister Maureen. The article claimed to "reveal the possible defense strategy of defense attorney Anthony Palermo, that it was rape and its emotional effect that led to the tragedy."

Palermo, a bit red-faced, admitted that he had talked to the magazine reporter about the case but denied ever saying the baby was conceived by rape.

Well, maybe not, but he had written that the conception was not the product of "any romantic relationship." If not romance, then what? Although it is possible to have consensual sex without romance, it is unlikely. Even one-night stands often feature sparks of romance, albeit brief.

At the beginning of February 1977, Sister Maureen, wearing a gray dress and a pair of large sunglasses that she never removed, attended a hearing at the courthouse during which she signed a jury trial waiver. This meant that there would be no jury. The judge alone would determine the outcome of her case.

The move was the defense's idea and the district attorney's office consented.

Judge Haas, who'd been with the case from the start, said that, though it was true that he'd read some of Sister Maureen's grand jury testimony, he had not passed judgment in the case and would have no problem going into the trial with an open mind.

Sister Maureen then left the courthouse, still hiding behind her shades, a woman so difficult to see.

The trial began on February 16. Valentino delivered the prosecution's opening statement, accusing the nun of giving birth to a full-term baby boy at around noon of the day in question. But when she heard another nun coming into the convent, she knew her secret would be out if the baby cried. She knew she was going to have to do something.

As she would throughout the trial, Sister Maureen listened quietly with a composed countenance. Spectators looking for signs of emotion were disappointed.

"After nine months of pregnancy, after nine months of continually hiding that pregnancy and dodging questions about her condition, after lying to other nuns about going to a doctor, now, seeing the baby alive before her, and now hearing the baby begin to cry, in this state of extreme emotional disturbance she thrust a pair of panties down the baby's throat as far as she could."

"Objection, your honor," Crimi said. "These accusations are unproved."

"Sustained. Mr. Valentino, please stick to the known facts of the case," Judge Haas said.

Valentino went on to say that Sister Maureen, after rendering the baby still and quiet, "discarded" the child in a waste paper basket, which she then placed behind a bookcase in an attempt to hide it.

Valentino said the baby was found and the reality of the situation was explained to Sister Maureen, she repeatedly denied that there was a baby or that she had ever been pregnant, a viewpoint that must have been difficult to maintain as she delivered the placenta in the hospital emergency room.

Charles F. Crimi delivered the defense's opening, explaining that Sister Maureen was legally insane when the alleged crime took place, that she had lost so much blood during childbirth that she had lost her ability to distinguish and appreciate the difference between right and wrong. Indeed, she didn't then or now understand fully what had occurred.

Spectators, of course, couldn't keep their eyes off of Sister Maureen, who sat calmly, close to still, as she listened to both opening statements. Sitting behind the defendant were several nuns from Sister Maureen's order, there in support of both her and their superior who was scheduled to testify that day.

Interestingly, the defendant, her family, and any nuns in attendance were allowed to use the courtroom's backdoor, the one usually used only by the judge, court attendants, and the lawyers.

Unlike most trials held in Monroe County, this one was being covered by newspapers and periodicals across the country, most controversially by *Ms. Magazine* for a planned sociological discussion about the possibly detrimental effects of celibacy.

When Crimi finished his statement to Judge Maas, the judge asked the prosecution to call its first witness.

The prosecution began its case by putting two Brighton police officers on the stand, to establish that a crime had been committed, that a baby had been found and the death of that baby appeared to be homicide. They then called Sister Kathleen Carroll.

"You are Sister Maureen's superior, Sister Kathleen?" Valentino asked.

"Yes, at Our Lady of Lourdes convent," Sister Kathleen replied.

"How many nuns live in that building?"

"Twelve, counting me."

"And you are in charge of them all?"

"I am."

"Now let me direct your attention to the morning of April 27, 1976. Did you receive a phone call that morning?"

"I did."

"From whom?"

"Sister Maureen. She said she had severe intestinal pains and would not be able to teach school that day."

Sister Kathleen said that a few minutes later she went to Sister Maureen's room to check on her. She entered the room and saw Sister Maureen bending over and she had a towel in her hand. At first Sister Kathleen thought that Sister Maureen was vomiting.

"I asked her if she was all right and she said she was, that she was just under the weather but it was getting better and she hoped that she would be able to make it into school for the afternoon."

"What time was this?" asked Valentino.

"About five minutes to eight in the morning."

"How long did you stay in Sister Maureen's room?"

"Only a minute or two. I had to get to school myself."

"Did you, at that time, know that Sister Maureen was pregnant?"

"I did not."

"Do you ever speak to your nuns about personal matters?"

"To some I do, some I don't."

"Had you noticed that Sister Maureen had put on weight?"

"Yes."

"When did you first notice that she had put on weight?"

"Around Christmas—Christmas 1975."

"Did you ever speak to her about it?"

"No."

Sister Kathleen testified that she returned to Sister Maureen's room after school. She opened the door and found Sister Maureen lying in a pool of blood. She was wearing an orange bathrobe and it was soaked with blood.

"What did you do, Sister Kathleen?" Valentino asked.

"I asked her if there was anything I could do. She apologized to me. She had promised to call at noon if she wouldn't be able to make it to work, and she told me she was too weak to call."

"What did you do when you saw all of that blood?"

"I called out for someone to call an ambulance."

"And someone did?"

"Yes."

"Do you remember who?"

"No."

"What did you do after the ambulance was called?"

"While we waited I tried to get Sister Maureen cleaned up. I got some of her legs cleaned off but I didn't get very far. And then the ambulance attendants arrived and took Sister Maureen out. They told us she was going to Genesee Hospital."

"How did Sister Maureen appear as she was being taken out?" Valentino asked.

"She was pale and shaking."

Sister Kathleen testified that she went immediately to Genesee Hospital, burst into the emergency room, and found Sister Maureen on a stretcher. Sister Maureen said she was waiting. They wanted to take her into surgery to see why she was bleeding. They thought it might be her kidneys or something.

"I asked her when she last had her period," Sister Kathleen testified, as she was convinced from what she had seen that Sister Maureen's problems were gynecological.

Sister Maureen told her she had last had her period a month ago, so maybe that was it. Maybe she was having her period.

Sister Kathleen didn't think that was the case at all, but she said nothing that might upset Sister Maureen, who seemed very weak.

They took Sister Maureen away and Sister Kathleen spoke to a doctor. He said that Sister Maureen had had a baby, and it must still be back at the convent.

"He sent Sister Jean and myself back to the convent to look for…" Sister Kathleen needed a moment. "To look for it."

It took a while but Sister Kathleen finally managed to testify that they had found Sister Maureen's baby, not alive, in a fetal position in an orange wastepaper basket that had been pushed behind a bookcase.

"We, we, we had to move the bookcase to get to the wastebasket," Sister Kathleen said.

Five other nuns testified that day. And their stories fit

together perfectly like a jigsaw puzzle. This was partly due to their inherent honesty, being nuns and all, but also to the fact that they had probably rehearsed their lines in advance.

Sister Barbara said she'd known Sister Maureen for eighteen years and had never seen anything, in Sister Maureen or any other woman, like the weight gain Sister Maureen experienced before she had her baby. Sister Maureen was normally quiet but she thought her even quieter than usual during the months while her belly grew.

"You saw Sister Maureen's room after she was taken to the hospital?"

"Yes."

"Could you describe what you saw?"

Sister Barbara said on the floor there was an orange bathrobe soaked with blood, a large pool of blood on the floor, and two rugs and three bath towels also blood-soaked.

The prosecution then introduced the orange bathrobe into evidence, and there were gasps as it was no longer orange, but the ugly purple brown of long congealed blood.

Sister Barbara concluded her testimony by describing a conversation she had with Sister Maureen four months after the baby was born.

"What did she tell you about the birth of the baby?" Valentino asked.

"She said that she heard Sister Rita coming in from school, and that she tried to call out to her, but she was too weak and she guessed Sister Rita didn't hear her. She said that the child was born in the bathroom and she remembered carrying him to her bedroom. That's down the hall from the bathroom."

Crimi cross-examined Sister Barbara and established that Sister Maureen did not remember the child crying.

"Did she tell you that's all she could remember? Up to the point where she brought the child to her room?"

"Yes."

Sister Jeanne Morrell said that she returned to the convent

at 2:55 p.m. and went into the bathroom, which was splattered with blood.

"What did you do?" Valentino asked.

"I went to Sister Kathleen and told her something was very wrong," Sister Jeanne said.

Sister Rita Jongen, a teacher at Corpus Christie School on East Main Street, testified that she returned from school to the convent around noon, a distance of approximately three miles, to "brush her teeth." She said she didn't see Sister Maureen, and heard no sounds coming from Sister Maureen's room.

The only indication that there was something wrong was the footprints. There were footprints on the rug in the hallway heading to the bathroom. At the time Sister Rita only registered that they were wet footprints. Later, she realized that they were bloody footprints.

"In the months before all of this happened, Sister Rita, did you notice physical changes in Sister Maureen?"

"Yes, she was growing very large in her stomach."

"Did you ask her about those physical changes?"

"I did. I asked her what was up and she said that when she put on weight it was always right in the stomach."

The next day, Dr. Ralph Sperrazza testified. He was one of two obstetricians that treated Sister Maureen when she was brought to the hospital. He said that Sister Maureen had a "normal womb," and that, according to physical and chemical tests, she didn't suffer from either of the two disorders that might endanger the life of a newborn child. She suffered from neither a hypertensive pregnancy nor placental issues.

The other obstetrician, Dr. William Grace, largely repeated the earlier testimony. Under cross-examination Dr. Grace admitted that there were disorders that Sister Maureen might have had, such as a pinched umbilical cord, which he could not rule out. There was no way to determine if the baby had bled to death after the umbilical cord was cut.

"When you treated Sister Maureen, did she understand why she was there?"

"Objection, your honor, calls for a conclusion not within the witness's expertise."

"Sustained."

"Did she say to you that she understood why she was there?"

"No, sir. She expressed confusion. She said she thought she might be having her period."

"She admitted to no knowledge that she had given childbirth?"

"For the first day she was in the hospital she denied knowing she had been pregnant."

On February 24, the prosecution countered any notion that Sister Maureen was confused about the reproductive process and was somehow taken by surprise when she delivered her baby. To do this, they used Sister Maureen's own words. Valentino read aloud from Sister Maureen's grand jury testimony, a read-back allowable because it contained admissions relevant to the trial.

Sister Maureen said: "About November I became aware of the fact that I was with child. I knew through my weight gain and because I no longer had my menstrual periods, and in December I felt the movement of the child within me. And I planned right from the very first sign of awareness to have the child and to keep—to keep him, to deliver him in a hospital. I worried very much during the last months of my pregnancy about not getting medical help, except that I hoped and prayed that he would be healthy. I didn't think that out of the whole origin of the problem that the Lord would let me down, and also I counted on the fact that because I am generally a very healthy person that the baby would also be healthy."

Sister Maureen was asked if she ever discussed her pregnancy with any of the other nuns at her convent.

"Yes, yes, I did. They were concerned about my weight

gain, and also about my legs, my legs were swollen, and I told them that I had talked to a doctor about, uh, fluid retention."

"Had you talked to a doctor about fluid retention?"

"No."

"Have you ever had a discussion with anyone about the retention of fluids?"

"No, but I have read about it."

"Do you remember what you wore to sleep in the night before you gave birth?"

"Yes, I was wearing a blue nightgown."

Of course, the blue nightgown had ended up tied around the baby's neck.

"After the baby was born, did you hear any sounds?"

"No. I recall the fact that his arms moved but I didn't hear him cry. And I can remember being distressed, but in a muddled way, and I can remember thinking in a muddled way, 'Why doesn't he cry?'"

This, of course, contradicted what she had said to doctors in the Genesee Hospital emergency room: "What baby? I'm a virgin."

When Valentino finished reading the excerpt from Sister Maureen's grand jury testimony, grand jury stenographer Lois Corbett took the witness stand to verify the accuracy of Valentino's read-back.

Dr. George Abbott, the deputy Monroe County medical examiner, who had performed an autopsy on the baby, testified that the baby had been alive at birth but had been gagged and asphyxiated until he was dead. A pair of white panties caused the gagging. Those panties had been stuffed as deeply as was physically possible down the baby's throat.

During Crimi's cross-examination, Dr. Abbott was asked to discuss the possibility that the child was stillborn, and responded that he was "reasonably certain" that the baby was alive.

"The lungs would have looked different than they did if

the baby had been stillborn," Dr. Abbott said. "There was air in the lungs, stomach, and intestine."

The prosecution's final witness of the day was State Police Investigator George Thompson who testified that he had attended the baby's autopsy and saw Dr. Abbott pull five or six inches of cloth material from the baby's throat.

On Friday, February 25, the prosecution rested.

"Mr. Crimi, are you ready to call your first witness?" Judge Maas asked.

"We are, your honor. The defense calls Dr. Stephen Dvorkin."

Dr. Dvorkin testified that he was the first psychiatrist to treat Sister Maureen after she delivered her baby. He saw her at around 10:00 p.m. on the night she was brought to the hospital.

"How would you describe her demeanor at that time, Dr. Dvorkin?"

"She was distant and detached."

"Were her emotional reactions normal in any way?"

"No. In fact, she didn't seem to be reacting emotionally at all."

"After your examination did you come to a conclusion as to why the baby died?"

"I did. I believe Sister Maureen killed her baby because she felt guilty."

He said he believed her when she said she remembered giving birth but she didn't remember killing the baby, that a combo of guilt and blood-loss contributed to a pair of mental disorders that took over the nun's mind during childbirth and during the next few days that followed.

"What were those disorders, Dr. Dvorkin?"

"Neurosis and psychosis."

"And what was the effect of those disorders on Sister Maureen's memory?"

"For a few days she didn't remember that she'd been

pregnant, much less giving birth and the aftermath."

"Would those disorders cause a change in Sister Maureen's behavior?"

"Oh, yes."

"In what way or ways?"

"She would be out of control and capable of performing abnormal acts. The blood loss would aggravate that condition, making her unable to cope with the usual stresses in life."

"Now, would you say that Sister Maureen was experiencing the usual stresses?"

"Oh, no. Being a nun, being pregnant, and all of that came to the moment of delivery and had an explosive impact on her."

"When did Sister Maureen's amnesia begin to lift?"

"About three days after she came to the hospital. She remembered being pregnant and became tearful and sad-eyed as the reality of what had happened sunk in."

"Was there a time when her amnesia further lifted?"

"Yes, on May 18. I had not seen her for a couple of days and when I came to visit she said that she'd had a breakthrough and could remember more things, including the hours just before she gave birth."

"Did she describe those events to you?"

"She did. She told me she remembered waking up at about three in the morning with cramping pains. It didn't occur to her that she was going into labor because her own estimate had it that she wouldn't deliver until sometime in May. She told me that later that morning she began to bleed heavily and made several trips down the hall to the bathroom and back. She told me that she made a concerted effort to clean up after herself, but she was bleeding a lot and didn't do a very good job. She was very worried because she didn't want the other nuns to return and find a mess. She said she once called out for help to another nun but apparently she didn't hear her. She said there was a phone in the hall and she tried to make a phone call but she fell on her way there and the call was never made."

"What did she recall about the childbirth itself?"

"She said she recalled delivering the baby in the bathtub on top of a pink mat. She remembered picking up the baby and carrying him back to her room."

"Did she remember seeing the baby move?"

"Yes."

"Did she remember hearing the baby cry?"

"No."

"Does she remember anything further about the baby?"

"No, after that she doesn't remember touching the baby or hurting it in any way. She doesn't remember putting the baby down, placing the baby anywhere."

"Does she remember other events following childbirth?"

"She remembers falling down again and bleeding more. She says that the memories she has are weird because she felt as if she were no longer in the same body."

"Was she fully conscious at this point?"

"I don't believe so. I believe she was slipping in and out of consciousness until she was discovered by the other nuns," Dr. Dvorkin concluded.

"Are you still treating her?"

"I am."

"No further questions."

The emotional highlight of the trial came the following Tuesday, March 2, when Anthony Palermo called Sister Maureen to the stand to testify in her own defense. For her big moment, Sister Maureen wore a raspberry-colored turtleneck sweater with a gray skirt and vest. Around her neck was a gold chain and cross.

Palermo asked the defendant if during the time she was pregnant, she had thought ahead to what she would do after the baby was born.

Sister Maureen said she had: "I did consider the possibility of adoption, but my strongest inclination was to keep him and to do that I knew I would have to leave the congregation."

With a small smile, she admitted to keeping her pregnancy a secret, but she knew that there would come a time when her secret would inevitably become known.

"Why did you keep your pregnancy a secret?"

"I wanted to spare my family and friends and members of the religious community from the suffering I knew they would undergo if they knew."

"Did you change your manner of dressing during the pregnancy?"

"No, I wore slacks outfits normally when I teach."

"You knew there would come a time when you could no longer keep your pregnancy a secret, correct?"

"Yes, when my labor pains began I planned to ask someone to take me to a hospital."

She added that those plans went awry when she didn't recognize her labor pains for what they were. She had figured it out and had determined that the baby's due date wasn't until May 10, still two weeks away.

"I had gone to the library and read pre-natal books, plus I had spoken to women who had had babies, and the intense, constant pain I was experiencing that morning wasn't like the labor pains I had learned about. When I awoke in pain at about three o'clock that morning I thought it was probably intestinal pain, or maybe the flu."

Sister Maureen testified that, although she'd been up since three with pain, her bleeding did not start until about nine that morning.

"Did you think about calling for help?"

"Yes."

"Did you call for help?"

"No."

She said that, once she started bleeding, she made several trips from her room down the hall to the bathroom, and that at one point she got into the tub so she would stop making a mess everywhere, and perhaps she would better be able to clean herself off.

"A few minutes later I became aware it was impossible to wash off the blood because I was in a pool of it. Sometime thereafter I suddenly felt a pain, very low, and also characterized by a bearing-down pressure. My water broke. I became aware at that moment I was about to deliver my child."

"What did you do then?"

"I got out of the tub and just knelt down on the bath mat and delivered the child. I carried the baby and the bath mat back to my bedroom."

"How far was your bedroom from the bathroom?"

"About thirty-five feet."

"Was the baby moving?"

"Yes, I remember his arm moving."

"Did he make any sound?"

"I don't remember him crying."

"What do you recall?"

"I recall crossing the threshold of my room. I fell…"

"Do you recall doing anything to the infant after carrying him to your bedroom?"

"No, Mr. Palermo, after that I don't recall anything about the child at all. I don't recall seeing him."

"Did you intend to harm or hurt the child in any way?"

"No."

"What is the next thing you remember?"

"I remember being found and being taken to the hospital. I sort of remember being asked questions by the doctors in the emergency room."

"What do you mean by 'sort of'?"

"Well, I didn't have any control. The words felt like they were coming out of a different person."

"No further questions," Palermo said.

On cross-examination, Valentino asked her how she knew what to expect when she went into labor. She replied that she had read about it in pre-natal books that she kept secretly in her room.

"You say your water broke. Didn't you know at that point that you were about to give birth to a baby?"

"Yes," she said, and suddenly sounded rehearsed. "But you also have to consider what was taking place in my mind because of the loss of blood. You can't separate one from the other."

She apparently meant that her amniotic fluid and blood were mixed together and that she didn't keenly distinguish them.

"Why were you so interested in cleaning up the bedroom and bathroom?"

"I don't know. I only know that it was one of my thoughts."

Valentino then read aloud from Sister Maureen's grand jury testimony, during which she said she was embarrassed by the mess she was making and that she "knew the effect it would have" on the other nuns in the convent.

"You knew right from wrong at that time, didn't you?"

"Yes."

Sister Maureen had been on the witness stand for two and a half hours.

That afternoon Dr. Robert Greendyke, a former Monroe County Medical Examiner, testified that he had performed an autopsy on the body on June 11 and the request of Sister Maureen's defense team.

He determined that the infant could have died from blood loss. To be more specific, he explained, the child could have died of an oxygen deficiency in the womb because Sister Maureen lost thirty to forty percent of her blood that morning. Or, the child could have bled out after birth because his umbilical cord was not clamped.

"Were the child's lungs fully inflated?"

"No, they were not."

"Could the baby have been stillborn?"

"Yes."

On cross-examination Valentino asked Dr. Greendyke if the baby could have died because it had cloth stuffed deep into his throat. The former county medical examiner conceded that that was another possibility.

The defense's final witness was Dr. William Libertson, who testified that he had examined Sister Maureen several times in an attempt to get her to remember those crucial moments after she gave birth.

He said that she made a "tortuous effort" to recall but could not. All she could do was "weep convulsively." She did however come to grips with reality, telling the doctor that she must have been the one to hurt the baby because she was the only one there.

"Does Sister Maureen feel remorse?"

"Oh, absolutely. She told me it didn't make any difference if she was imprisoned because of her actions. She felt imprisoned by her mind and heart because she could not escape from her thoughts."

Predictably, the psychiatrist said that Sister Maureen's mental disorders made it impossible for her to intend to harm her child.

The prosecution had suggested that Sister Maureen would not have been able to walk around if she had been in shock from blood loss, but Dr. Libertson said that wasn't true.

"That can happen," he said.

"Did you ask Sister Maureen if she had ever considered having an abortion when she learned she was pregnant?"

"I did ask her that, yes. She told me that she never considered that an option because she felt abortion was unnatural."

"Did you ask her if she could imagine choking a baby and putting it in a wastebasket?"

"I did. She said that she had heard stories of babies being left, but she herself could not imagine doing that. She said, and I quote, 'I am thirty-six and not naïve.' I asked her if she could explain what happened and she said, 'If I didn't plan to hurt him before he was born why would I plan to hurt him after?'"

The defense rested its case at that point but the prosecution called a witness in rebuttal, a Dr. Michael Lynch of Buffalo who testified that enough of Sister Maureen's brain was functioning for her to "understand her actions," that she "knew and understood the consequences of her actions on the day the baby died."

On March 3, both sides delivered their closing arguments for Judge Maas. Crimi argued on behalf of the defendant, and became emotional during his oration.

"Sister Maureen is a girl who, since the age of seventeen, has devoted her life to children. Judge, I cannot conceive of this girl killing anybody. The prosecution has failed in its efforts to demonstrate that Sister Maureen intended to kill the baby. Please take into consideration, your honor, that having a mental defect is a legitimate defense against first-degree manslaughter charges," Crimi said. "And please recall that the prosecution failed to demonstrate that Sister Maureen killed the baby at all, that there was no way to know for sure that the baby was not stillborn."

Valentino's tone on behalf of the people was colder, more business-like. His point was that, just because the defendant was a nun didn't mean she wasn't a liar—or a killer.

"First thing, your honor, there is evidence that the baby was not stillborn. There was air in his lungs and the defendant herself testified that she had seen the baby's arm move. She remembers this, she remembers that. We are being asked to believe that the defendant remembers *everything except* how the baby was asphyxiated and left in a wastebasket. That's amnesia of the most convenient kind. What we heard here, your honor, was a well-rehearsed ten-month fabrication supported by psychiatric excuses. The facts clearly demonstrate that the defendant, upon hearing another nun entering the building, with her baby crying or about to cry, stuffed a pair of panties down the child's throat and asphyxiated him," Valentino said.

He went to his table, picked up a photograph of the dead baby, and approached the bench with it. "This photo screams out to you, to you as a judge and a human being, for common sense and justice in this case."

Following the arguments, Judge Maas announced that in addition to the first-degree manslaughter charges that would result in a mandatory prison sentence, he'd consider lesser charges such as second-degree manslaughter or criminally negligent homicide, both of which did not carry mandatory prison sentences.

Judge Maas retired to his chambers to deliberate.

At 11:00 a.m. on March 4, 1977, Judge Maas declared Sister Maureen not guilty of all charges. The courtroom was silent as Judge Maas announced his verdict, with the exception of one member of the gallery, a relative of the defendant, who let out a single short cry.

As the news sunk in there were the sounds of sobs from the gallery behind the defendant. Sister Maureen covered her face with her hands and cried. Quickly pulling herself together she hugged and thanked her attorneys.

Judge Maas did not explain his reasons for reaching the not guilty verdict. He announced his decision and left, going directly to the Rochester airport where he caught a plane for Boston. Even when reporters did track him down, he refused to make a comment.

One nun from the gallery was overheard saying, "We knew she didn't do it," a statement that blatantly misrepresented what had just occurred.

Attorney Anthony Palermo said that he and his client were not surprised at the across-the-board acquittals. Had a deal been made? If so, it was never publicized.

Valentino begrudgingly took questions.

"Why was the father never identified?"

"His identity was irrelevant to the child's death."

"Do you know the circumstances around the child's conception?"

"It happened while Sister Maureen was on vacation in August 1975."

The Sisters of Saint Joseph issued a press release stating that they were grateful that the "ordeal" of the trial was over. Sister Maureen would be living at an undisclosed location and could remain a member of the order if she chose to—for the time being.

Later, Sister Mary John, representing the order, said, "This has had consequences and it will have consequences. The order will wait to see what happens next. At the moment we are too close to the situation to comment further. We can hardly believe that the case is finally completed."

District Attorney Lawrence Kurlander commended Valentino for prosecuting the case with "competence and dignity. It was not a case we looked forward to, but we were obliged to prosecute under the law. Right from the outset, I thought it was a case of great tragedy," Kurlander said.

On her way out of the Hall of Justice, Sister Maureen shook her head when asked if she had anything to say. She slipped her tiny self into a seemingly oversized car and disappeared back into the cloud of anonymity from which she had briefly emerged.

And the story, too horrible to tell, was seldom told until Rochester all but forgot it had ever happened.

The case was turned into a thought-provoking novel, *Unholy Child* by Catherine Breslin (1979); a Broadway play, *Agnes of God*, written by John Pielmeier (1982); and a film of the same title (1985). And decades later, there were many Rochesterians who remembered these, especially the movie, but had no idea that the actual tragedy occurred in Brighton.

Looking southeast, the stone culvert as it appeared in 1922, two years after the body was found. Judging by the height of the water, best guess is this photo was taken in the spring.

MOSQUITO POINT ROAD

Until the middle of the nineteenth century, farmers on the west side of the Genesee River in the town of Chili had to take their goods northward seven miles to the city and then come back down just to travel by horse-drawn wagon to a house or store on the other side of the river. On October 14, 1859, Chili Supervisor O.L. Angevine presented a petition signed by three-hundred Chili residents demanding a bridge be built to connect northeastern Chili with West Brighton and Henrietta to the Monroe County Board of Supervisors. In response to the petition, the Board passed a resolution calling for a bridge to be built, 215 feet long and sixteen feet wide, resting on a pier to be built in the center of the river. The resolution was passed on December 16, 1859, and the bridge was built. It was called the Ballantyne Bridge after Anna Ballantyne, the Chili farmer behind the petition. That bridge only lasted for fourteen years. In 1873 it was removed because it was determined to be "unfit for public use." Using the mid-river pier already in place, a new bridge went up, which lasted until 1913, at which time the third span was constructed, a twin to the iron trestle that allowed the West Shore Railroad cross the Genesee a quarter mile to the north. Charles F. Stowell, an Albany bridge expert, designed the bridge. The bridge was completed on May 1, 1914, and lasted until 1961. The road, now called Ballantyne Road, was then known as Mosquito Point Road, and one of the first persons to live on it was James Harper, who owned the land at the Rochester and Pittsburg Railroad (now Baltimore & Ohio) crossing. He moved there in 1910, and recalled that Mosquito Point Road would become two feet deep with mud when the spring waters receded. In 1920, the road became well known to city dwellers because it was the site of a famous murder, about which you are about to read. Four years later, Harper suggested that, to rid the dirt road of its undeserved stigma, the name be changed to Ballantyne Road, as it led more or less to the Ballantyne Bridge on its easternmost end. Those brave enough to live on Mosquito Point Road, and for the first twenty-five years it was known as Ballantyne Road, mostly remember the floods, which were an annual adventure. Only after the Mount Morris dam was completed in 1952 did the stretch between Scottsville Road and the Pennsylvania Railroad tracks south of Genesee Junction become populated.

On January 8, 1920, shortly before noon, the body of a young man wearing only his underwear was found stashed on the ice under the stone trestle just north of Mosquito Point Road. The trestle, a culvert originally built as an aqueduct, crossed Black Creek near the Genesee Junction turntable. The location was described to city dwellers as "just south of Britton Field" which was the one-year-old airstrip that would grow in stages into the Rochester International Airport.

The bridge took the Pennsylvania Railroad across, just south of where that line crossed the West Shore Railroad at the Genesee Junction station. This is the same bridge, known in my neighborhood growing up as the "trussle," i.e. trestle, and sometimes as the "aqueduct," a throwback to a time when the Genesee Valley Canal crossed Black Creek. It was stone and looked permanent, with two tunnels just high enough so you could canoe under it if you limboed back so as not to hit your head.[2]

In 1920, even main roads in Monroe County looked like this one, dirt and well rutted.

The man under the trussle had been stabbed, horribly slashed, disemboweled, his skull caved in, and, most disturbingly, his head had been skinned. His scalp was flayed, his ears shredded. Only a slim thread of cartilage kept one ear

[2] The trussle was where George-Ann Formicola and Kathy Bernhard were last seen swimming before being murdered and horribly mutilated with a knife, forty-six and a half years later, subject of my book *The Devil at Genesee Junction*.

on his head.

The body was discovered by chance by a member of the crew of train 9333 of the Pennsylvania Railroad who caught a glimpse of the body as his train was crossing the trestle. The engineer notified the Monroe County Sheriff and the body was removed from the ice by order of Coroner George Killip.

On the banks of Black Creek next to where the body had been stashed, sheriff's investigators found two sets of footprints, one male, and one female. The sheriff himself said that it was the most brutal murder he had seen around those parts in a very long time. The heaviest muddy shoeprints from the woman were found under a tree about sixty feet away from the body, where there was also a large patch of red snow. Resting atop the body was a wooden club that appeared to at one time have been part of a railroad tie. There were bloodstains on it, and it was presumed this was the big stick that put the hole in the body's skull.

Nearby they found the heel from a woman's shoe stuck in the mud. An investigator looked at those female prints and envisioned a woman dancing about in distress as she watched a man being killed in a gruesome way. As it turned out, he had it all wrong.

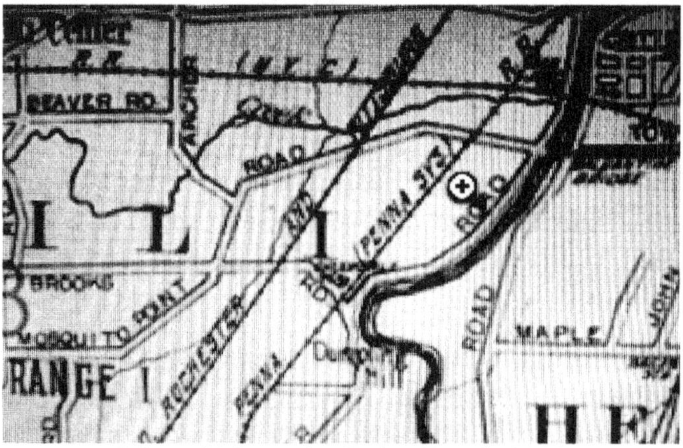

Map of Mosquito Point Road, 1922

Investigators agreed that there must have been an extended attack because it would take tenacity and a special kind of anger to flail that much skin off of a man.

They found evidence (broken foliage) suggesting a violent struggle. In the weeds beside the railroad tracks they found pieces of the handle of a revolver. The chamber of the gun, a .32, was found near a tree. It appeared to Sheriff Andrew Wiedenmann that the assailant had used the revolver to pistol whip the victim, hitting him with the gun until it broke.

All of the evidence near the Genesee Junction was photographed *in situ* by William Meagher of the police Bertillon department.

The sheriff was horrified. He decided then and there that he was going to work this crime until the perpetrators went to the electric chair, for nothing else would be suitable punishment for what happened to this victim.

Reporters, then known as "pressmen," in downtown Rochester were intrigued and knew something was up, something that would sell newspapers, when they saw young women being brought in for questioning.

A big break in the case came when a taxicab driver working for the Ford Taxicab Company, a Charles H. Scherer, called up police headquarters and said he thought he might have given the victim and his killers a ride out Scottsville Road as far as the Ballantyne Bridge.

Sheriff's detectives picked up Scherer at his home and took him to the morgue, where they showed him the body. The driver looked, winced, and then said yes, that was the guy in his cab. With him during the ride was a young couple.

They asked him if he had any clue as to the identity of the killer couple. He thought about it and said he'd overheard them talking about a man named Arnold who lived on North Washington Street in the city. The man, who naturally seemed in charge, said he needed a cab to get out to the country because his own car had developed engine trouble. The man asked Scherer to take him out to Mosquito Point Road and at first Scherer didn't want to do it.

"Why didn't you want to do it?"

"Well, for one thing, the other man and the young woman were handcuffed together."

"Why did you take the fare, then?"

"He flashed a badge and said he was a detective from police headquarters."

"How much was the fare?"

"Two-fifty." That is, $2.50.

Two employees of Gleason Works came to the morgue and said they wanted to look at the body. They worked with a guy who had been abducted and wanted to see if he was the victim.

"Yup, that's him," they said.

"What's the guy's name?"

"Edward J. Kneip." Pronounced Nipe. "Sometimes he goes by the name Ed Knight."

"He has an alias?"

"Nah. People just hear it wrong, so he got used to going with it."

Police found a George B. Arnold on Richmond Street, a millwright, and he turned out to be the stepfather of James Louis Odell, known as Jimmy Odell.

"Jimmy have any issues with anyone?"

"Well, yes," Arnold said.

Arnold said Jimmy had been incensed as of late because his teenaged wife Pearl was "outraged" before their marriage by some scoundrel.

"What was the guy's name?"

"Ed Knight."

Ed Kneip, police learned, was a young machinist at Gleason's who was the sole support for his widowed mother Mary and sister Josephine. There had been an embarrassment for him at work the previous week when someone called up his workplace and said Kneip was wanted by police for rape. Minutes later, a man showed up at Gleason's and asked to see Kneip.

Pearl Beaver Odell

An all-points bulletin went out. Wanted for suspicion of murder were Jimmy Odell and his wife Pearl. Police thoroughly searched Arnold's home and found Pearl, but James wasn't there.

They also found a fur coat and a woman's skirt spattered with blood. There were two suitcases fully packed and ready to go—but obviously left behind.

"Why did you kill Kneip?" they asked.

"He had it coming to him," was all she would say.

A neighbor came running over to the Arnold house and informed police that they'd just missed Jimmy Odell.

"I saw him running out the back door just as you were arriving," the neighbor said.

Police located Odell a few blocks away walking down the sidewalk casually. He broke into a run when he saw he was surrounded, but they nabbed him.

The Odells were hauled in together and questioned separately. District Attorney William F. Love and Sheriff

Wiedenmann took turns vigorously interrogating Jimmy and Pearl Odell.

Ballantyne Road, just west of the old Genesee Valley Canal bed, looking west, sometime in the early 1990s.

They quickly confessed to killing Kneip. Jimmy said he used an old gun to help keep Kneip prisoner. The joke was on Kneip though, because the gun was useless, wouldn't shoot. But it did its job, and later they used it as a weapon, to pistol whip Kneip.

Jimmy and Pearl were arraigned on January 9 before Monroe County Judge Willis K. Gillette. Attorney Elmer Shaffer was retained to defend the Odells. The young couple had been kept apart since their arrest and greeted each other in a subdued fashion when re-united momentarily in the courtroom.

Odell trembled and beads of sweat popped up on his face, but he spoke up loud and clear. He alone was responsible for Kneip's demise, so there was no point in them holding his wife for one second longer. She didn't have anything to do with it.

His plea was ignored and both were arraigned on first-degree murder charges. In stark contrast, Mrs. Odell remained calm and silent. They waived a preliminary hearing in lieu of evidence being evaluated by a grand jury.

The Odells were separated again and taken back to their cells. Though both had been advised by Shaffer to keep their mouths shut, Pearl was eager to chat when visited in jail by a reporter.

"I was an innocent girl of sixteen until I was wronged by Kneip," she said. "When I first met him on Christmas Day in 1918, I thought he was a good fellow. Five days later I had the bitter experience of knowing I had been deceived. Even then I would have forgiven him had he kept his promise to marry me. He did not do so. Instead he made indecent proposals. It was then and there that I broke off keeping company with Kneip. Later in the summer I began to go with Mr. Odell and found him to be the opposite of the other man. Kneip told some very unfair things about me. Some of the stories were absolutely untrue, and it was only reasonable that they came straight back to me. They were cowardly. Yes, I told my husband all about the affair before we were married on December 15th last."

So the Odells had only been wed for about three weeks.

"He forgave me for my part in the matter, for I had not offended," Pearl said. "Naturally we talked about it, and my husband grew more and more incensed."

The reporter found Jimmy in a talkative mood as well. He repeated what he'd said in the courtroom. The blame was his, all his.

"They ought not to keep my wife locked up. I don't believe they can convict her, can they? Kneip was the cause of Pearl's troubles. No one knows what I suffered on his account. Why, every time I walked down the street I imagined the people were sneering at me and smirking all the while. 'Your wife has been out with other fellows,' I could almost hear them saying."

He admitted that his wife had told him all about Kneip and he had forgiven her.

"But I kept brooding over what had happened to her. I tell you it was on my mind day and night. It kept me awake sometimes until late in the night, just thinking that some other man had wronged her."

He said that Pearl first told him about Kneip in a short letter in which she said that she felt her life was "blasted" and was considering suicide.

Kneip, Jimmy said, had attacked Pearl while she was alone in her boarding house, where she should have felt safe. When Odell couldn't take it any more, and sought Kneip out, and met Kneip for the first time ever on the occasion of Kneip's death.

Kneip worked at Gleason's Tool Work on University Avenue, and Odell went to see him there. Odell identified himself as a police officer with a warrant charging him with rape.

In retrospect, Odell figured Kneip must have known nothing about the law, because he went like a lamb, got into a cab with Odell and didn't even ask questions when Odell drove south out of the city and into the country.

"He never asked me who I was," Odell recalled with amazement. "When I told him he was accused of rape, he asked who was the accuser. I told him Pearl Beaver and his face turned red and I knew then he was guilty. He knew someone had something on him. She was under age when he outraged her."

Odell said he asked the cabbie to pick up his wife and she rode with them. Kneip kept quiet. Odell crossed the river at South (Genesee Valley) Park and drove out of the city on Scottsville Road. The cab dropped them off on Mosquito Point Road, just north of the Ballantyne Bridge.

Odell walked Kneip along the Pennsylvania railroad tracks that crossed Mosquito Point Road, heading north alongside the old bed of the Genesee Valley Canal. Odell pulled Kneip out of the car and "handcuffed him to a tree." He said that his wife was there and she was carefully observing, but she did not participate in any way.

Once Kneip was helplessly attached to the tree and defenseless, Odell turned to Pearl and said, "Pearl, if this man ever did anything wrong to you then go ahead and do what you want to with him."

James Louis Odell

Pearl pulled out a large metal file and went to work on Kneip. She started by beating him in the head and face with the file.

Kneip's screams of *"Pearl! Pearl! Pearl!"* were loud at first, then weak, and then he was silent. She hit him in the head until Kneip was unconscious.

Odell said they thought Odell was dead so they uncuffed him from the tree and rolled him down the embankment toward the edge of the creek.

Odell moved in closer to adjust the position of the body when Kneip, who'd been playing possum, sprung at him. Kneip was choking Jimmy.

That brought Pearl back into the action. She went at him again with the file, hitting him on the head with it until he was out. Then she removed his clothes lustfully and used the file to scrape at him hungrily. Odell said he couldn't look and turned away as his wife brutalized her rapist.

When she had had her fill, when her bloodlust was quenched, she slumped into exhaustion. Her husband wanted to make sure the scoundrel was dead this time and bashed his head in completely with the big piece of hickory from a railroad tie.

They dragged the semi-nude corpse under the bridge, but not all the way under. They were out of strength and stomach, and eager to get away from the body.

They gathered up the man's clothing, which they tossed behind a fence. Then they walked back to the city, first south toward Mosquito Point Road, east to Scottsville Road, and north to Elmwood Avenue, South Avenue and to their home on Griffith Street.

When Odell's mom learned that her son had confessed to murder, she broke down and from her knees wailed, "Oh, my boy, my boy, my boy, I taught you to be good, why did you do it?"

Pearl's confession agreed with her husband's with one exception. She remembered something that her husband had either forgotten or edited out for taste. Pearl said that after Kneip was dead, she grabbed his trousers, which were nearby, and she pulled his knife out of his pocket. Then she stabbed him in the belly and ripped with all of her strength until Kneip's intestines spilled out.

Police asked Pearl about the packed suitcases they had found at her stepfather's house. She said that the plan was to flee to Pennsylvania that night, but they didn't get the chance. Instead of leaving, they delayed their departure with plans to return to Genesee Junction and bury Kneip's body.

Police asked Pearl what she did with the shoes that lost a

heel at the crime scene. She said that she burned them in the backyard as soon as they got home.

Authorities believed the parts of the confession that they wanted to believe and disregarded the rest. They thought the idea that Kneip had played possum while being skinned alive was absurd.

It was funny. They admitted doing it. But went out of their way to lie about the methodology. She claimed to use the file only as a club, when the evidence is clear that she also used it to grate the skin off Kneip's body.

They never did explain why they stripped off Kneip's clothes. It didn't seem to serve a practical purpose. The sheriff was no mind reader, but it seemed sexual. The motive was sexual, they were slaying a rapist, and perhaps there was a point when the crime was planned to be more sexual than it turned out to be.

On the evening of January 8, police received a call from a Mrs. Names, who lived on Mosquito Point Road. When she heard about the murder, she called the sheriff and said that she'd seen a touring car the night before discharging passengers near her home. It got her attention because it was not a highly populated area and it was unusual for someone to get out of a cab out there.

With Jimmy Odell in custody, two Gleason's employees were brought in and positively identified him as the guy who pretended to be a detective at the factory to pick up Kneip.

A reporter found Mrs. Ellen Arnold, in whose house the Odells' packed bags had been found. She said that James Odell was a good boy who had been greatly imposed upon. She explained that her Jimmy was a Rochesterian born and raised. He had never had an opportunity to graduate from high school because of his health. At age seventeen he enlisted in the National Guard, was transferred to the Naval Militia, and served aboard the *Columbia*, and remained in the service until the previous year, 1919. There were unconfirmed rumors that Odell was discharged early because of "mental deficiency."

She said that Jimmy Odell was a Mason, an Odd Fellow, and also belonged to other fraternal organizations. She said that Jimmy met Pearl Beaver when she was only fifteen and the family lived on Flora Street, just south of Corn Hill between Plymouth and Exchange streets. She called at the house accompanied by her sister. Mrs. Arnold remembered that the young girl had braids down her back. They, of course, didn't see each other while Jimmy was in the Navy, but reunited in August 1919. Mr. and Mrs. Arnold went on a motoring trip and took the young couple with them. After that Jimmy and Pearl kept steady company. Both Arnolds stood up for Jimmy and Pearl when they were married on December 15, and the Odells moved into the Arnold's house.

"You ever hear of this guy Kneip, Mrs. Arnold?" the reporter queried.

"Oh yes, in March of 1919, Pearl told me she was going to marry Kneip. Later, she lied, embarrassed I guess, and said that she actually had married Kneip, and she showed me some silver presents that she claimed had been given to her by her new husband. She didn't see Pearl again until August of 1919, when the girl admitted that she hadn't actually gotten married."

Mrs. Arnold was asked about the murder and volunteered that the file Pearl used on Kneip had been hers. "It was good and sharp too," Mrs. Arnold said, "I had just had it sharpened to cut ham. Last I saw of it, it was in my kitchen sink. She must have grabbed it on her way out."

On the night of the attack, Odell had picked up Kneip at his work and brought him to the Arnold house where part of the drama played out with Mrs. Arnold as a witness.

"I heard Jimmy ask Kneip if he had ruined this girl. Kneip denied it but Pearl cut in and screamed that he knew he did it, he knew very well that he did it. Kneip complained that he never promised to marry Pearl. Kneip said something to the effect of, 'Take me to the Court House and I will tell you all.' Kneip didn't know that Pearl's husband was questioning him. He still thought he was talking to a detective of some sort. Kneip was looking for sympathy and turned to my husband and asked him what he thought about it. My husband told him it was his own fault, that he was an adult and he should have known better. No sympathy there.

"Pearl, Jimmy and Kneip then left, and Pearl must have taken the file from the sink with her. Jimmy and Pearl didn't get back until about one-thirty the next morning. I was in my room. Pearl came in and she said, 'Mother, I've done it. I did it alone. Jimmy didn't have anything to do with it. I slammed him.' She said that Jimmy told Kneip that they were going to see Pearl's mother, and then that they were going to go to a place where they could have it out and not be interrupted. Pearl said that she thought the two men were going to have a fistfight and that would be it. She said that they took him to a place way out in the country and Jimmy grabbed Kneip by the throat, squeezing so hard that Kneip's eyes were bugging out and his tongue was hanging out. That was when she hit Kneip with the file. She said she took Kneip's gold knife out of his pocket and stabbed him in the abdomen with it. She said that Kneip fell to the ground and she kicked him in the face. She said she kicked him so hard that she broke the heel off her shoe. She told me they dragged Kneip and put him under the culvert, and then returned home. Now they had to pack their bags and get away as soon as possible. They were heading toward Pennsylvania."

The *D&C* located Pearl's sister, Mrs. Terrance Cosgrove, who lived on Elba Street in the city.

"What was your sister like?" the reporter asked.

"She was always wild," said Mrs. Cosgrove. "Still, I was shocked when I learned of the tragedy. I hope for the best. Pearl's evil ways have finally gotten her into trouble. Pearl came here to Rochester from Elmira about four years ago. She was destitute. She worked for a time in the Rochester Button Company's factory. And then at the Art-In Buttons Company. When she came to Rochester she lived with me. She and I argued for the most part. She had developed many bad habits, of which swearing was the least—but she sure could swear. I tried to get her to stop because of my twelve-year-old daughter. I told her if she didn't cease with that type of conduct, she would have to leave. The worst thing was not the swearing. It was the young men she kept bringing around. Eventually, the young men became too much for me and I asked her to take other accommodations."

The reporter asked if she knew the victim in the recent tragedy. Mrs. Cosgrove said yes, Mr. Kneip was one of the men that Pearl had brought around when they were housemates.

"He was a splendid fellow," Mrs. Cosgrove said. "One night he called and my sister was away, so Kneip and my husband sat on the back porch talking until about ten o'clock. At that time Pearl called and explained that she had found a new job and was going to be home late. Kneip left and that was the last time I ever saw him."

"How well do you know Jimmy Odell?"

"Not that well. When he started seeing Pearl he drove a car and he didn't come in. He waited for her to come out. Then they went away and got married. Not long after that Jimmy did come over to my house. He was angry. Someone had told him that Pearl and Kneip had gotten married earlier in the year and that they had gone away together on a honeymoon to Washington and Pennsylvania."

"What did you say to that?"

"I told him that it was hogwash. I guessed he'd heard it from one of Pearl's girlfriends. Pearl likes to make things up to make her life seem exciting. It was probably just one of the lies she told."

"What do you think happened to Kneip?"

"She put him up to it. It was her idea and he went along

with it. Mr. Cosgrove thinks so as well."

As this was going on George Arnold wanted to set the record straight. It had been reported in the paper that he "had no use" for Odell and he wanted the world to know that this wasn't true.

Originally from Yates County, but a Rochesterian for twenty years, Arnold said he'd known Odell for six or seven years, since Jimmy was a boy, and he felt as if he'd become "sort of a father" to him.

"I tried to develop him into a true man," Arnold commented. "I cannot understand it. Nothing was ever said in the house that indicated that either Odell or his wife planned to do anything to young Kneip. In fact, they never spoke of him in my hearing."

Arnold didn't think Jimmy had violence in him. "When he was in (the town of) Painted Post three years ago, the boy attended the Baptist Church regularly. He was baptized in that church, sang in the choir, and acted as an usher."

Kneip's funeral was held on Monday morning, January 12. The body was laid out inside a closed casket at the Kneip home on Caffery Street. The funeral was at Saints Peter and Paul's Church with Rev. J. Emil Gefell celebrating the high mass. There was an unusually large attendance for the service. Every pew was filled, with many of the attendees being strangers attracted to the case by the publicity.

In charge of the arrangements was the Loyal Order of Moose, of which Kneip had been a member. The pallbearers were fellow members of the lodge.

If you eliminated the lodge brothers and sympathetic strangers, there were only a few friends and family members left. Among them were Kneip's mother, his sisters Josephine, who lived in the family home, and Mrs. George Proper of Middletown, Connecticut. An uncle, William Hoffman of Buffalo, walked Kneip's mom to her front-row pew. Kneip's fiancée Viola Williams of Gilmore Street, was there, plus a pair of cousins. The church's Christmas decorations were still up in sharp contrast to the solemn occasion.

A delegation from Kneip's lodge and workplace went to the cemetery with the body. Back in those days, the casket was routinely lowered into the grave as the loved ones looked on. The practice was discontinued because family members were often overcome with grief, and that was what happened here. Kneip's mother's knees buckled and she needed to be supported by Kneip's lodge brothers as she wailed, "Oh, it's all over."

The District Attorney's Office had no intention of letting the dust settle and announced they would immediately begin issuing subpoenas for grand jury testimony.

Pearl had a history of telling fibs based on the way she wished things were rather than on reality.

D.A. William Love summoned Dr. Wallace J. Herriman,

physician and alienist (psychiatrist), a former Rochester resident who was then serving naval duty in Virginia, to return to his hometown and interview Odell and his wife in anticipation of an expected insanity defense.

On the other side, the accused were being represented by Elmer Shaffer, who also wanted a physician to take a look at the jailed couple. His doctor was Dr. Edward L. Hanes, a neurologist on the staff of Rochester General Hospital. Hanes had served as a medic during World War I, and was considered an expert in mental cases. Shaffer announced that it would be the defense's contention that Odell had always been mentally abnormal and thus was not fully responsible for his actions.

The papers often referred to the killer couple as James and his "girl-wife." The nature of her defense was still unclear. Her motive was clear enough, and there was nothing mentally deficient about it. She had allegedly been raped and was fearful that Kneip's bragging about the taking of her maidenhead would effectively ruin her "happy home."

Reports from jail were that Pearl didn't appear overly bothered by her predicament. She was reportedly cheerful, and had a healthy appetite.

On Tuesday, January 13, the grand jury began hearing a parade of witnesses. Testifying on the first day were the Arnolds, Sherer the cab driver, Edward Spinks, described as Sherer's companion, and Mr. and Mrs. Jerome B. Names, who ran the gas station/convenience store at the Ballantyne Bridge and heard an automobile stop near their house on the night of the murder, the railroad crew that discovered the body and the coroner's staff who performed the autopsy on Kneip.

(For you history buffs, there is now a street that runs parallel to Ballantyne Road one block to the south, which at one time went east as far as Scottsville Road across from the then-location of the Ballantyne Bridge. It is Names Road, named after Jerome B. Names.)

In the jail, Pearl was claiming to be pregnant. A doctor, Dr.

Nathan Gorin, was sent to the jail to verify if Pearl was with child, but although she repeated her assertion, she refused to be examined. There were reports that her father and brother would be coming to Rochester from their home in Lopez, Pennsylvania, but so far they had not arrived. Pearl told her jailers that she had expected them to arrive by now but her father had said he was too sick to travel.

Sheriff Wiedenmann announced that he was looking into the policy of liberally distributing deputy's badges. It was disturbing to him that Odell had been able to spirit Kneip away from his workplace using such a real badge. The sheriff announced that he was ordering his office to make a master list of all such badges that had been given out so that they could be recalled.

Wiedenmann's predecessor, acting sheriff George Brown, had distributed hundreds of deputy badges during his nine months in office following the death of Sheriff Harley Hamil. During those nine months there had been labor disputes and strikes, and the badges were given out to factory watchmen and security guards in an attempt to keep the peace.

"There's no telling how many of them have fallen into irresponsible hands," Sheriff Wiedenmann said. The badge Odell used had not been found. The sheriff urged that anyone in possession of a badge to turn it in, and warned that anyone using the badge would be arrested for impersonating a peace officer.

On January 15, Pearl's mom came to visit her in jail, and almost broke down as she spoke to her daughter through a screen. Her husband David Strasser took a vacation so the woman could pay the visit. Also visiting Pearl that day was her sister Eva. The visit lasted for about a half hour.

Pearl's jailers noticed that the only time she revealed negative emotion came when her sister was visiting her. The young women cried together, a change from Pearl's usual upbeat manner.

It took Pearl's family two days to travel from Summer Hill, Pennsylvania. They spent the night in Olean, New York, before continuing northward to Rochester. While the mother and stepfather were at the jail, the jailer Raymond O'Loughlin served them with subpoenas.

The mom explained to the D.A. that she had been separated from Pearl's father for fifteen years and married Strasser in 1911. Now she wondered if that didn't have something to do with the jam Pearl found herself in.

When Pearl's parents separated, they broke up the siblings, with Percy, Minnie, and Millicent going with mom. Pearl went with dad and grew up on a farm in Lopez, Pennsylvania.

It was after talking to the district attorney that Pearl's mom finally gave out. She had to lie down in an anteroom before she could continue with her day. After she felt sufficiently strong to leave she was escorted to an elevator to be lowered to street level. Inside the elevator car she cried out, "This is terrible. I have never ridden in an elevator before."

Jimmy's mother was creating her own scene. She announced that she was declaring war on all reporters because everything they were publishing in the newspapers was untrue.

"Did attorney Elmer Shaffer tell you not to talk?" the guy from the *D&C* asked.

"No, he did not," Mrs. Odell replied.

That same reporter, who apparently had *cart blanche* in the jailhouse, asked Pearl a few questions as well.

"Were you glad to see your mother?"

"Yes, I hadn't seen her in years."

"How long?"

"I hadn't seen her since I left Pennsylvania three years ago."

"Why did you leave your father in Pennsylvania?"

"He had his arm taken off in a mining accident and I

thought it was time to go out and make my living."

"How old were you when you left home?"

"Fifteen."

"How far did you go in school?"

"I was just starting high school when the accident occurred to my father."

"Have you heard anything of your father lately?"

"Yes, he is sick in Lopez. And so is my brother Percy. But I expect him to come to Rochester at any time. As soon as he is well he will come to me."

"Mrs. Odell, did you know that the grand jury rose this afternoon?"

"No, I did not. What did they do?"

"They returned a murder indictment."

"First degree?"

"Yes, first degree. For you and Jimmy."

This startled Pearl, and she paused before she again spoke: "Well, all I can do is face my charge. I thought it would be so and I am not surprised."

"Mrs. Odell, according to two of your friends…"

"Which two?"

"Mollie and Aretha Ryman of Spring Street."

"Oh…"

"According to them, you ran away with a man when you were living in Colley, Pennsylvania, and you married him. Is that true?"

"No! Such a thing never happened. Please put it in the paper that I never did such a thing. Now that I am in this fix they will say all kinds of things to condemn me."

Pearl's next visitor was her father, William Beaver. He arrived at the jailhouse on January 17. After his visit he said that he had not seen his daughter in four years, ever since she left home for Elmira and then Rochester to look for work.

Pearl's mother went back home on the 17th without ever seeing her ex-husband.

The Odells were arraigned in Supreme Court on January 31 before Justice John B.M. Stephens. Both pleaded not guilty to the murder-one charges.

Female murder defendants were few and far between, so much attention was paid to what Pearl wore in court: a "becoming" hat that "perched" atop her head, a blue cape, and patent leather shoes. Some noticed that during her time behind bars she'd put on a few pounds and looked "stouter" than when she was arrested.

It was originally hoped that their trial would begin on February 16, but their attorney Elmer Shaffer said it would take him longer than that to prepare his defense.

Asked by Supreme Court Judge Robert F. Thompson when he might be ready, Shaffer said probably not until April. He had another murder case to defend and that was going to occupy his time until the spring.

Judge Thompson decided that there was more than one defense attorney in Monroe County and there was no reason why Shaffer should defend them all. He allowed Shaffer to remain in charge of Jimmy's case, but re-assigned Pearl's case to Louis E. Fuller, another defense attorney experienced in murder cases.

Pearl didn't like the idea, wanting the same defense her husband got. That ideal slipped further away when she learned that she and her husband were not to be tried together, that her trial would start as soon as his ended.

On April 7, Pearl announced that she wanted nothing to do with Fuller as her attorney. Only hours later she said she hadn't made up her mind. Her jailers were beginning to wonder exactly what did go on in Pearl's mind, as it often seemed a little crowded in there.

Fuller said that he was "indifferent" to what Pearl thought of him, and was prepping for her defense as per Judge Thompson's wishes. On April 8, Fuller visited Pearl in jail and came out a half-hour later saying she'd agreed to allow him to

Looking southeast, the old Genesee Valley Canal bed off Mosquito Point Road, with the Pennsylvania Railroad tracks to the left, where James and Pearl Odell handcuffed their victim to a tree and beat him to death.

defend her. Shaffer and Fuller said that their separate defenses would be "fully cooperative" with one another.

Pearl told a reporter on April 11 that she was hopeful she would be allowed to testify on behalf of her husband at his trial, but she added that it was Fuller's call. No one except Pearl thought her testimony on behalf of Jimmy's defense was a good idea. It was unclear how her testimony could help her husband.

Jury selection for Jimmy Odell's trial began on Monday, April 19, and was accomplished in a single day. Almost the full pool of 150 men was questioned before the twelve spots were filled. The jurors included a wood worker, cashier, receiving teller, passenger agent, saw maker, salesman, trimmer, laborer, laboratory assistant, civil engineer, paymaster, and a chemist.

During *voir dire*, Odell was flanked on one side by Deputy Sheriff Ed Fosmire, and Shaffer on the other. Also sitting at the defense table was Shaffer's associate Hampton H. Halsey. Sitting behind him were his wife, and the Arnolds, his stepmother and stepfather. Pearl sat next to her own guard, Deputy Sheriff George Leake.

Spectators noticed that she joined in the conversation when the choice was made whether or not to accept a juryman. When she shook her head no, the juror was not taken, and when she nodded he was, leaving the uncomfortable impression that she was to some degree calling the shots.

The fashion police were on top of the action. Pearl was wearing "a blue cape with a green flapping collar, which was thrown open as she sat in the courtroom. Underneath the cape was a Georgette waist with hand-worked rosebuds on it. She wore a black straw hat with a little bit of green with two rosebuds in front. On her feet were patent leather pumps."

This was possibly the same outfit she'd worn for her arraignment. It would figure that the teenager lacked a large wardrobe.

Her "large black eyes seemed to have a timid look as she watched the proceedings." Whenever she spoke with a man her eyes began to twinkle and she'd smile. However, there was "a snap" in her eyes when she looked at the prosecuting attorney.

Sitting on the prosecution side were Kneip's mother, two of his sisters, and his girlfriend Viola Williams. Spectators noted that the Kneip contingent seemed far more interested in the Odells than in anything the lawyers were saying or doing. They kept their vengeful eyes on the couple throughout.

By the start of the trial, interest in Rochester was so intense that people gathered along the street between the jail and the court, hoping to catch a glimpse of the Odells as they were taken to and from the trial. Jimmy and Pearl, on the other hand, seemed oblivious to the curiosity seekers.

The courtroom would be packed throughout the proceedings, standing room only—and unlike other popular trials of the day, more than half of the spectators were women.

The most mournful persons in the courtroom were the

stepmothers, Mrs. Arnold, who dabbed at her eyes with a handkerchief during the jury-selection process, and Mrs. Beaver, Pearl's stepmother. Both amped up their weeping whenever Kneip was mentioned, and let out a long moan when they first saw the large file Pearl had allegedly used to scalp and flay the deceased.

The defense was interested in jurors who thought a man defending his wife's honor was justifiable in his actions, no matter how violent. The prosecution was looking for jurors who were suspicious of expert testimony, especially of the alienist variety.

Odell wore a blue-serge suit with a soft collar and a dark tie. He wore horn-rimmed glasses.

There was a table at the front of the courtroom, upon which were displayed the prosecution's exhibits, including the file and the clothes—cap, undercoat, overcoat—Kneip wore on the night he was killed. Also exhibited was the bloodstained plush coat Pearl had worn that night.

On April 21, District Attorney Love delivered his opening statement, saying: "The prosecution's theory is that both Mr. and Mrs. Odell belabored Mr. Kneip as he was manacled to a tree. We will show that the handcuffs were removed from the deceased only after he had been beaten into insensibility. With the cuffs off he was rolled down the bank. There was some anxiety as to whether Kneip was really dead and they went down the bank to see. Earlier in the evening at the Odell home Kneip was questioned as to what his relations with Pearl had been."

The prosecution's first witness was Dr. Irving Harris who performed the autopsy and graphically described the condition of the corpse, covered as it was with bruises, cuts, and scrapes.

"What was the cause of death?" Love asked.

"It could have been one of two things," Dr. Harris replied. "Blows to the head or a punctured lung."

Florence Scherer testified that Odell had posed as a detective and wanted her brother to take his party—that is Odell, his wife, and Kneip—into the country. Her brother did arrange to give the trio a ride, but the witness was concerned about Odell's claim to be a deputy and called the police to let them know what was going on.

Charles Scherer took the stand and talked about that automobile ride. He took the trio to the corner of Scottsville Road and Mosquito Point Road and began to turn right when Odell stopped him. "We can walk from here," Odell said.

On cross-examination, Shaffer's associate Hampton Halsey asked, "At any time during the ride did you hear Kneip protest?"

"No, sir."

A series of witnesses were called, briefly interviewed, and excused, establishing that Odell had purchased a pair of handcuffs before the murder.

The next witnesses were Sheriff Wiedenmann, Railroad Detective Eugene Weller, and Deputy Sheriff Herbert Brockway, who described the discovery of the body.

The sheriff testified that when he first saw the body, still at the spot where it had been discovered, the deceased was wearing only underwear and a shirt.

"The right leg was drawn up and the right arm was against the side of the culvert. A burnt log lay on the left side partly on the cheek and partly on the shoulder of the body."

"Sheriff Wiedenmann, did you move the body?"

"I did not."

"Who was the first to move the body?"

"Coroner Killip."

The sheriff said that there was a lot of blood. It was scattered in the snow, and there was a pool of blood at the base of a tree that was later determined to be the one to which Kneip had been manacled.

"What else if anything did you notice around the base of that tree?"

"I saw two sets of footprints. One appeared to be from a man, the other from a woman. The woman's footprints showed that one of her shoes had a heel and the other didn't."

"Anything else?"

"Deputy Brockway found a watch in the snow in that same area."

"Did you follow the footprints?"

"I did. They went along the bottom of the canal bed to the culvert. It looked as if the two people had walked side by side and had dragged something between them. The weeds between the two sets of footprints were trampled down and the snow was disturbed."

"I show you now a piece of wood that is burnt at one end. Do you recognize it?"

"I do. We found that at the scene. We believe it was used to hit the deceased over the head."

"What if anything did you find in a field to the west of the scene?"

"I found the cylinder of a revolver, close enough to the scene to have been thrown there."

Detective Weller testified that he found part of the handle of a revolver at the scene.

"By that do you mean the rubber grip?"

"Yes, sir."

Weller testified that other items he personally discovered at the crime scene included a chain, a knife, a pair of handcuffs, and the previously mentioned pocket watch.

Deputy Brockway testified as to the discovery of the metal file, with bloodstains on it.

"How long was the file?"

"About eighteen inches?"

"Is this the file you found?" Again, someone in the gallery moaned.

"Yes, sir."

Brockway then testified regarding Odell's arrest, which was made by himself and Deputy Leo Sipple, as well as the search of the Arnolds' home during which Pearl's bloodstained coat was found.

"Is this that coat?" Love asked, holding up the exhibit.

"Yes, sir," Brockway replied.

"Deputy Brockway, when you arrested the defendant, was he wearing eyeglasses?"

"No, sir."

The next witness was Henry Saucke, who had at one time employed the deceased. He testified that, early on the day of the murder, Odell paid him a visit.

"What did the defendant say to you?"

"He said he was looking for Kneip."

"What did you say?"

"I told him Kneip didn't work for me anymore, that he had taken a job at Gleason's. Odell then left and did not return."

Gleason Works employment manager Price Kinney testified that he spoke to Odell on the day of the murder, and that Odell was impersonating a sheriff's deputy, showing him a gold badge. Odell requested that Kneip be brought to him.

"Did he say why he needed to see the deceased?" Love asked.

"Yes, he said that Kneip was a wanted man."

"Did he say which crime Kneip was wanted for?"

"Yes, sir. He said he was wanted for rape."

"And what did you say to his request?"

"I told him that he would have to come back after six o'clock because that was when Kneip reported for work."

Kinney was cross-examined by Mr. Halsey, who asked, "Are you sure that nothing was said that that man wanted to continue improper relations?"

"No, sir," Kinney said.

The prosecution called Jerome Names to the stand. He identified himself as the proprietor of a general store on Scottsville Road and testified that several customers came into his store on the night of the murder. At about nine o'clock that evening he was standing by his store's window and saw a "machine" — that is, a car — stop. He couldn't tell if anyone got out of the car because the headlights blinded him.

"Have you ever seen the defendant and his wife before, Mr. Names?"

"I have. On the Saturday before the murder I saw them on foot on Scottsville Road walking south near Britton Field," the witness said.

The jury was left to speculate what this was about. Were the killers out scouting locations for their eventual crime? If so, this was an indication of pre-meditation.

A Raymond C. Sparnon took the stand and corroborated Names' testimony. He said he was driving on the Scottsville Road on Saturday, January 3, when he saw the defendant and his wife on foot.

He remembered it well because he considering stopping and offering them a lift.

"Did you give them a ride?"

"No, sir."

"Why not?"

"I was carrying a load and there would have been no place for them to sit."

William Scheffel was next up. He told the jury that he operated a saloon in the city of Rochester at the corner of South Avenue and Griffith Street. He wanted to make something clear, it used to be a saloon, but since the Volstead Act he sold only non-alcoholic beverages. No one believed this to be true, but didn't challenge Scheffel.

The saloon-owner testified that on the night of the murder the defendant came into his bar. He did not initially order a drink, however. Instead he asked for a bucket of water for his automobile. He gave him the water. Odell left and returned and asked for a refill. Returning a second time with the empty bucket, Odell asked for a glass of cider.

Odell left the front door open and was letting the heat out. Scheffel asked him to close it and Odell said, "Excuse me. I don't want to let a party get away from me."

Odell took the glass of cider outside with him, returned after a few minutes with the empty glass and asked if there was a garage nearby.

He didn't close the door this time either and Scheffel had to move from behind the bar and close it behind him. As he did so he saw the man's car parked in the street, but he couldn't see it well enough to know if it contained passengers.

The afternoon's first witness was William R. Lansing, a court stenographer who was present during the confessions of both Odells on the night of the murders. His direct testimony served to enter a transcript of Odell's confession into evidence.

On cross-examination Halsey asked him, "Where was the defendant's statement taken?"

"In the sheriff's living apartment in the jail."

"Who was there?"

"Sheriff Wiedenmann, Brockway, Coroner Killip, Sipple, District Attorney Love, and Love's assistant James O'Connor."

"Did he have an attorney at that time?"

"He did not."

"Did anyone say anything to him as to what his rights were?"

"Not that I know of."

"Was he told that he did not have to make a statement unless he wished to?"

"I don't recollect."

"Or that it would be used against him?"

"I don't recollect."

"Your honor, I request that the confession be taken out of evidence as it was not a voluntary statement."

"Request denied," the judge ruled. "Mr. Love, you may read the confession to the jury." After the reading, the prosecution rested its case.

On Wednesday, April 21, not only was the courtroom

packed, but also there were an estimated three-hundred people in the corridors of the courthouse wishing against hope that a seat might come available during the day. Pearl Odell took the stand in defense of her husband and was sworn in.

Before the questioning began, Judge Thompson warned the gallery, in particular the female spectators, that the testimony they were about to hear would likely be an embarrassment to sensitive ears, and anyone who didn't want to be subjected should leave.

No one budged.

"Proceed," Judge Thompson said.

"Good morning, Mrs. Odell," Halsey said to the witness.

"Good morning," she replied with a serious face.

"Could you please tell the court where you were born?"

"Yes. In Lopez, Pennsylvania."

"Shortly after you were born your parents separated and you were sent to live with another family?"

"Yes. When I was fourteen years old I was forced to go to work."

She added that she worked at various places in or near Rochester, and that she was living with a family on Judson Street when she became acquainted with the victim in this case.

"Do you remember on which date you met Mr. Kneip?"

"Yes, it was Christmas Day, 1918. He bought me a box of chocolates. I ate some, but I noticed that he refrained from doing so."

"What happened after you ate the chocolates?"

"I became dizzy and passed out."

"You became unconscious?"

"Yes, sir. When I came to I was on the couch. When I realized what had happened to me I told him he would have to marry me. I said if he didn't I would have him arrested. He said he would marry me and we fixed the date for February 28, 1919."

"Did you marry Mr. Kneip on that date?"

"I did not."

"Why not?"

"He asked me for a postponement of the wedding because he was not working. There was a postponement to May and then another to June. Before the June date arrived Mr. Kneip made a revolting proposal to me and I told him I would have nothing further to do with him."

She testified that in August 1919 she and James Louis Odell began to keep company. He proposed to her in December 1919 but she told him she could not marry him because she had had illicit relations with another man.

"Were you and the defendant living separately when he proposed marriage to you?"

"No."

"What were your living arrangements?"

"We had been living together as man and wife in the house at number 106 Adams Street for about two weeks when he proposed."

There was a collective gasp in the gallery, and Pearl blushed.

"I turned down his proposal and soon thereafter wrote Jimmy a letter stating that I would kill myself because of my previous relations."

The defendant, she said, forgave her for what had happened and she agreed to marry him. Only after they were wed did Pearl give her husband the identity of the man who had drugged her chocolates and taken advantage of her. At that time, she said, they were living in the home of Mr. and Mrs. George B. Arnold of Richmond Street.

"And who are the Arnolds?"

"They are my husband's stepparents."

"What happened after your husband forgave you?"

"He continued to worry about what had happened to me. He would get up in the middle of the night and pace for an hour or two. When he was in that state of agitation he couldn't lie abed."

"Did there come a time when Mr. Kneip tried to get in touch with you?"

"Yes, sir."

"When was that?

"December 20, 1919."

Pearl testified that Kneip contacted her and said he wanted to see her. She met him on Main Street just west of Fitzhugh Street and proudly told him that she had married Odell and therefore could not go around with him.

Kneip told Pearl that she should go around with him despite the fact that she was married to another man, and if she didn't he would write a letter to her husband and to her place of work telling them what had happened, only he would leave out the part about drugging her chocolates.

Pearl testified that she told the defendant all about Kneip's threats and suggested that Odell go see Kneip where he worked, to bring him to their home, and to make him confess the truth about his relations with Pearl. Odell agreed to do just that. (The implication here is that Odell did not necessarily believe Pearl regarding the story of the chocolates and his "forgiveness" may not have been as complete as she'd testified.)

Halsey pointed out that two witnesses had testified at the trial that they'd seen Pearl and her husband walking along Scottsville Road on January 3, theoretically scouting out locations to commit their crime.

"They are mistaken," she said firmly. "The first time we ever went out there was a few days later, we went by car, and we had Mr. Kneip with us," she said.

To solidify her alibi she said that on that Saturday when she was seen walking the road south of the city, she was actually taking her coat to the cleaners and buying phonograph records at a store on Main Street East.

Halsey decided to allow the jury to sort out that contradiction and moved on.

"Your husband brought Kneip home with him?"

"Yes, sir. He asked Mr. Kneip to confess, and Kneip said, 'Let her tell it.'"

"Did you tell it, Mrs. Odell?"

"Yes, sir."

"And what did your husband do?"

"Jimmy made Kneip put his hand on a Bible as he admitted it was true. My husband then said, 'Pearl, put on your hat and coat. We will take the automobile down to the police station.' So we took the automobile and headed out."

"Was there any talk of going to Scottsville Road or Mosquito Point Road?"

"No, sir."

"There was no talk of taking him to any other place?"

"No, sir."

"What happened next?"

"There was a mechanical issue with the automobile. We arrived at a saloon on Griffith Street and Jimmy went inside."

"He left you and Kneip alone in the automobile?"

"Yes, sir. And it was at that time that Kneip used an expression that I do not care to repeat here."

Mrs. Odell testified without a flicker of emotion, taking her version of that day's events right up until the moment of the attack, at which point her attorney Louis Fuller stopped her.

"Just a moment, if the Court please, may I address a remark?" Fuller said.

"You may," Judge Thompson said.

"I represent Mrs. Odell, who is charged with the same crime. While I thought it no more than fair that she should testify for her husband, I think that she should not proceed further."

The judge replied, "The law provides that no person can testify to any fact tending to convict the person of that crime. This is a personal privilege which may be determined by the witness." To Pearl he then added, "It is your privilege to refrain from answering or from giving any testimony which may help convict you. Counsel has made a proper objection, but you must decide."

Fuller said, "I trust you will follow the advice of your attorney?"

"Yes, I will," she said.

And thus it was Mr. Love's turn to cross-examine.

"On January 8, you were brought to the jail?"

"Yes, sir."

"Later on, you talked to me concerning this case?"

"Yes, sir."

"Did you tell me that Kneip ever struck you?"

"I don't believe I did."

"Up until that time did you know the deceased's name was Kneip?"

"I did not. I had always called him Knight. I thought that was his name."

"During the time before you broke relations with Mr. Kneip, did you meet any other members of his family?"

"Yes, I met his mother and sister. I believe that was on June 2, 1919."

"Is it a fact that on the night of June 2, Kneip came to your home and sat in the parlor and waited for you and you didn't come home but telephoned to a neighbor's home about being late?"

"No, sir."

"Was there ever such an occurrence?"

"There might have been."

"Isn't that the truth, Mrs. Odell?"

"No, sir."

"When did Odell propose to you?"

"The latter part of November or the first part of December."

"And at that time you were already living with him at number 106 Adams Street?"

"Yes. I told him I could not marry him because of my previous relations."

"And what made you change your mind?"

"I received a visit from Mrs. Arnold, who urged me to marry Jimmy."

"The whole matter of your relations with Kneip was gone over on the Saturday night before you married Mr. Odell, wasn't it?"

"Yes, sir."

"Isn't it true that Mr. and Mrs. Arnold believed that you were married to Kneip?"

"Yes."

"Did you say anything to anybody about being married to Kneip?"

"Yes, sir."

"Whom did you tell?"

"Mrs. Arnold. When I came back from a visit to Pennsylvania."

"Did Mrs. Arnold give you a wedding present at that time?"

"Yes, sir."

"Where did you tell Mrs. Arnold that you were married to Kneip?"

"When I was at the Arnold house."

"Did they ever call you Mrs. Kneip?"

"No. They always called me Pearl."

"As I understand it, you didn't see Kneip from June 2 until that Saturday in December when you met him?"

"Yes, sir."

"Did you know that your husband had a pair of handcuffs in the house?"

"Yes, sir."

"Did you know that he had a deputy's badge and a revolver?"

"Yes, sir."

"How did you know?"

"I saw them lying around."

"How long did he have those items, to your knowledge?"

"He had the revolver before we were married. He'd had

the handcuffs for three or four weeks, at least three weeks."

"Kneip was the first person to have improper relations with you?"

"Yes, sir."

"You've said you had improper relations with Kneip fifteen times, is that correct?"

"I know it wasn't any more than that."

Again there was a buzzing in the gallery, enough so that Judge Thompson pounded his gavel and gave the courtroom a good glare.

"When you left the Arnold house, did anyone grab hold of the handcuffs?"

"I don't know. Both my husband and Kneip went out ahead of me."

"You are pregnant, Mrs. Odell?"

"Yes, sir."

That did it. There was chaos in the courtroom. Judge Thompson pounded and admonished until he was blue in the face, but a full minute passed before order was restored. When it got quiet, it got very quiet. The questioning was not through and no one wanted to miss a word.

"How far along are you with your pregnancy, Mrs. Odell?"

"Five months."

You could practically hear the gears grinding as the gallery did the math. The baby had to be Odell's.

"You told the defendant about your improper relations with Kneip before you married him—isn't that the truth, Mrs. Odell?"

"Yes, sir."

"No further questions, Your Honor," Love said. Halsey had no re-direct and Mrs. Odell was excused from the witness stand. She returned to the gallery and sat between her lawyer and her guard.

The judge called for a fifteen-minute break so everyone

could regain his or her composure. The break ran a little long, but when court re-convened, a Mr. J. Greenhouse was called to the stand. He identified himself as the manager of the American Cloak Company. His testimony corroborated Mrs. Odell's claim that she was not traipsing around Scottsville Road near the air strip on Saturday, January 3, but had come into his store.

"She and her husband came in twice," Greenhouse said.

A James Bryan took the stand and testified that he was a lawyer, and the man who had sponsored the defendant's initiation into the Elks.

Bryan testified that he had been playing billiards with the defendant in the Elks Home one night when Odell told him a story that he now realized paralleled the truth.

Odell said that when he came home from the army he had a female cousin who said she had been raped. He asked if there was anything he could do about it.

"What did you do, Mr. Bryan?"

"I asked to meet the cousin, and the defendant brought Pearl to me, although I did not know her name at the time."

Pearl, Bryan said, continued the masquerade that she was Odell's cousin. She gave him the facts as to what had happened to her, and Bryan advised Odell and the woman that, in his opinion, he didn't believe "any conviction of rape could be had."

"Did you say anything else, Mr. Bryan?"

"Yes, sir. I added, 'It is unfortunate that something cannot be done. A man like that should not be allowed to live.'"

"And what did the defendant say to that?"

"He agreed with me. He said, 'A man like that deserves to be punished.' I told him the only chance was to get the man to confess in front of a reliable witness. My recommendation was that he go home and forget about it."

"What did the defendant say to that?"

"He said he would do as I said, that he would go home

and forget it."

"No more questions," Halsey said.

"Mr. Love?" Judge Thompson said.

"Yes, your honor. I have a few questions in cross-examination. Mr. Bryan, did you have any conversations with the Odells in which the word 'chocolate' came up?"

"No, sir."

"Was there any mention of the word 'killed'?"

"Yes, sir. Odell said, 'He ought not to be allowed to live. He ought to be killed.'"

The defense appeared as if they were going to wrap up their case with a couple of character witnesses.

Robert S. Axe, a bank bookkeeper, said he had known the defendant for four years and judged him to be of excellent character.

Frank Alexander, a printer, said he was in the Naval Militia with Odell. They had been stationed together at Pelham Bay, in the Bronx. He judged Odell to be of good character. Love did not bother to cross-examine either of those witnesses.

At that point, the feeling was that the defense would rest. But there was one more surprise.

"The defense calls James Louis Odell."

As the defendant moved to the front of the courtroom, the judge told the gallery that he was not going to make it voluntary any longer, he wanted all women who were not connected with the case out of the room. There was a protest, and a couple of women needed to be pried from their seat, but eventually the room was as Judge Thompson wanted it, and the direct examination of the defendant commenced.

Odell said that he was twenty-two years old. His mother died when he was nineteen months old. His father married the current Mrs. Arnold, the woman he had always known as his mother. He entered the Naval Militia in 1915, and the federal service in 1917. All in all, he had crossed the Atlantic

Ocean nine times. He received a medical discharge. After the service he worked in a factory, where he had an accident that cost him part of his middle finger. He met Pearl when she and her sister came to visit his stepmother. Pearl was always crying, which he believed at the time was because of an unhappy marriage. He thought she was married because she wore a wedding ring at one time. He said he did not have improper relations with Pearl until they lived together on Adams Street, which was after she said she couldn't marry him but couldn't tell him why. He later learned the reason, that this man Kneip had abused her.

"She told me she was doped, or she never would have done such a thing."

The questioning progressed to the day of the murder, how Odell had learned that Kneip worked at the Gleason Works, how he arrived at the plant at six in the evening and had to wait for Kneip to arrive.

"Had you ever seen Kneip before?"

"No, sir. In fact, I had to ask the timekeeper to point him out for me. As soon as Kneip reached up to grab his time card, I grabbed him…Oh, and by the way, I was not anywhere near Scottsville Road on January 3. Those witnesses were mistaken. I was at the YMCA early that day and in the afternoon I went to downtown Rochester with my wife."

Odell told the court that he had talked to Judge William C. Kohlmetz at the IOOF Hall and asked him if a conviction of Kneip could be obtained. The judge told him that a conviction would depend on corroborative evidence.

He said he purchased the handcuffs a couple of days before the murder, but the revolver had been his for years.

"The gun was rusty and I had no bullets for it," Odell explained.

Getting back to his story regarding Kneip, he said that after grabbing the deceased at the factory time clock, he put the handcuffs on him and took him to Pearl. He asked her if this was the correct man and she said yes. He asked Kneip if he wronged the girl, and Kneip said she should tell it, which she did. When she finished he admitted it was the truth. Odell made Kneip swear to it on a Bible. That done, he put Kneip and his wife into his auto with the intention of taking him to the police station, but his car stalled and he went into a saloon to get water for the radiator. He bought two glasses of cider, drank one himself and gave the other to Kneip. (The saloonkeeper had testified that Odell purchased only one glass of cider, but this seemed a minor point.)

"Did Kneip drink the cider?"

"Yes, sir. I then dragged him around to the back of a building and asked him if he thought he was a man when he bragged about wronging Pearl. He replied, 'She isn't any good. She's only a — —.'" Kneip had used a word or phrase that was unsuitable for print in 1920.

"What did you do then?"

"I told Pearl what Kneip had said about her and asked her what she wanted done. She said, 'Suit yourself.'"

After that, Odell testified, he couldn't get his car to start so he hired a car to take them out Scottsville Road. They sat in the back seat with Pearl on the right, Kneip on the left, and Odell in the middle. (This contradicted eyewitness accounts that Odell had handcuffed Kneip and Pearl together.)

"Did you say anything on the way out?" asked Halsey.

"No, sir. Not a word."

Halsey asked Odell about the large file that had been used during the killing. Odell admitted that he had it and said it was usually used when he changed tires on his car. (Mrs. Arnold had claimed the file was hers, and that Pearl had taken it from her sink before leaving the house. We are left to envision this eighteen-inch tool which can both "cut ham" and help change a tire.)

When they got to Mosquito Point Road, the driver let them out. They all got out the right side of the car, Kneip exiting last.

"Did Kneip protest?"

"Not a word."

"What did you do?"

"We walked down the road, Mosquito Point Road, although I didn't know the name of it then."

"Did you have anything else with you but the gun and file?"

"No, sir."

They turned right when they got to the old Genesee Valley Canal bed and walked until they came to a bridge. Near there, he handcuffed Kneip to a tree.

At that point Judge Thompson interrupted, noted the late hour, and adjourned court for the day. The Odells and their lawyers were asked to remain until the room had emptied. They were then taken out through the judge's chamber, led a back way into the basement, and exited the building through the portal usually used to take out the ashes from the coal furnace.

As Pearl was being taken out of the courtroom, she was overheard saying, "They might as well kill me if they give my Jimmy first degree."

One observer noted that she was still only eighteen years old, but they had been a hard eighteen years. She looked ten years older than she was.

The following morning, the crowding conditions both inside and outside the courthouse were drastically increased. The word had gotten out that testimony was juicy.

There were wrestling matches as men fought to get into the courtroom to watch. Outside the courthouse the crowd had grown until the sidewalks could no longer hold it. It spilled into the street and halted trolley service for a time.

On the witness stand Odell picked up his story where he had left off: "We had Kneip handcuffed to the tree. I said to Pearl, 'There he is. If what you say he did is true, there is your chance to punish him as he punished you.' Pearl took the file and went over to him. 'Eddie!' she said. 'You started me on my downfall.' 'You're nothing but a — —anyway,' Kneip answered. She hit him with the file. I hit him with the revolver and the revolver broke."

"What was Kneip saying during this beating?"

"All he said was, 'Oh Pearl, oh Pearl.'"

"What happened next?"

"She dropped the file and Kneip kicked it away. We walked away and intended to go home, when I thought of the letter he had claimed to have written, the letter that besmirched my Pearl's character, we went back to see if he had it on him. I reached into his pocket for the letter. He jumped up and hit me in the face. Then he caught me by the throat. Pearl grabbed him by the coat and pulled him off me. He chased her and I followed. He fell down and kicked up at me. He grabbed me. He had me part way down and was squeezing me by the throat. Pearl came up behind him. I don't know whether she hit him or not. I did not know what was going on. When I recovered myself Kneip was lying on the ground. Pearl was fixing her collar. Then we cut off his clothes as to hide his identity," Odell said, and then turning to face the jury, he added, "I swear to God I never intended to kill him."

With that, the defense rested.

Judge Thompson called for a fifteen-minute break, after which the jury would hear the closing arguments.

During his final argument on behalf of the defendant, Shaffer told the jury: "The highest crime that you can convict James Louis Odell of is manslaughter in the first degree. I hope to satisfy you that I am correct.

"It is a case of such importance that no man can exaggerate its importance. Each man on this jury has read something of the case. Each man has seen the crowds that have thronged the courthouse. Each man has seen the crowds that have been seated in the courtroom. This was a tragic affair, but I don't wish to have you think of me an apostle and disciple of crime. I want there to be in the city of Rochester the supremacy of justice.

"Gentleman, here is a young man whose character had remained with him. When he put that character before you no attack could wear it down. There has not been an attack on that character in any way by the district attorney. You can't punish a man for a crime unless you have overwhelming evidence."

At that point sobs could be heard in the gallery and all heads turned to see who it was. It was Pearl, completely broken down in her seat behind her husband. The defendant turned and tried to console his wife. After a brief pause, Shaffer continued.

"Believe me when I say this. My client loved his wife. He loved her—and he was a clean boy. There is absolutely nothing to say but that he is and was a good, clean boy.

"She said to him. 'I have done wrong and I don't want to drag you down. I can go on into degradation, as thousands of women have gone before me.'

"But the clean lad loved her, and love recognizes no other power. Before you could find this man guilty of murder in the first degree, you would have to violate the law of nature.

"I will say that my friend, Mr. Love, will be heartless in his mercy, and you will see that I am right. The whole purpose I have today in presenting this case to you is to make you see justice, and I say you cannot find this defendant guilty of more than manslaughter in the first degree.

"Pearl tried to commit suicide and Odell subsequently married her. In that one act he showed the faith that was within his breast."

Shaffer then hammered for a while at attorney James Bryan, who had testified that Kneip could not be convicted of a crime based on Pearl's uncorroborated statements. "He ought to have had Kneip arrested, arrested for the crime of rape in the second degree, as Pearl was less than eighteen years old. That would have meant ten years in Auburn prison, and none of us would be here today. Murder in the first degree? Ha! It is better that a millstone be tied around his neck and he be thrown into the sea. It is preposterous to call it a cold-blooded heartless murder.

"On the night that Kneip confessed the rape to the defendant, he sat there like the wilted dog he was. That wretch, that seducer, destroyed Pearl's innocence!"

With that both Pearl and Mrs. Arnold began in unison to sob loudly. Mrs. Arnold, a handkerchief held to her face with one hand, got up and left the courtroom. Pearl, of course, was under guard and stayed put.

Shaffer waited until the door closed behind Mrs. Arnold and turned again to the jury: "Right down to the last, Kneip called her the vilest names he could think of, and he spit in her face. And Odell did what any self-respecting man would do.

"Gentlemen, the only kind of mercy I want you to apply in this case is a just verdict. The only imaginable crime that this man is guilty of is manslaughter in the first degree. I conclude now by saying, give this man the benefit of the doubt. Treat it like men."

Judge Thompson waited a couple of beats and allowed Shaffer to take his seat next to the defendant before saying, "Mr. Love?"

"Thank you, your honor," the district attorney said. He rose and moved in front of the jury. "I charge this man with the crime set forth in the indictment, murder in the first degree. You are to search the entire record and find the truth, find it from the character, find it from the witnesses. When you go at this job you will go at it in that way. You are not to let sympathy sway you. There is no manslaughter here. This is murder in the first degree. Every slightest bit of evidence is one-hundred percent perfect. So I say to you, weigh it all.

"If ever there was a ridiculous story it was the one Odell told about the handcuffs, that he was going to use them at his lodge. A bit of comedy, gentlemen. Fine, fine, a fine bit of comedy.

"The defendant went to Mr. Bryan you'll recall and he told Bryan that such a man should not be allowed to live, that such a man should be killed. Is that premeditation?"

The district attorney gave a blow-by-blow description of the killing, of the brutality.

"They cut his stomach through to the liver," he said. "Imagine what must have been done to create the conditions that were found. The man must have been pounded and flayed, pounded and flayed, into insensibility at the tree. And then disemboweled! His skull was macerated. Did they go back after letters or did they wish to see if he was dead?

"In closing, I submit to the men that the evidence beyond all question bears out the charge in the indictment. Gentlemen, the proof does not demand that a murder second degree, or a manslaughter verdict shall be brought in, but a verdict of murder in the first degree."

Judge Thompson charged the jury and deliberation began at 10:30 a.m. on Friday, April 23, 1920.

At 5:45 p.m., the jury asked the Court to instruct them again regarding the difference between murder one, murder two, and manslaughter.

Judge Thompson said, "The killing of a human being is murder in the first degree when committed from a deliberate and premeditated design to effect death.

"Second degree murder was done with the design to effect murder but without premeditation.

"Killing is manslaughter in the first degree is when an attack is committed without a design to effect death, when in the heat of passion or by means of a dangerous weapon."

Although the jury didn't ask, the judge took the opportunity to explain again what was meant by "reasonable doubt." He added that if any juror thought a portion of any witness's testimony was not credible, they should reject some or all of that testimony. He reminded them that their job was to determine guilt or innocence. They were not to discuss possible punishment. That was his job.

The jury didn't say a thing. The foreman nodded and the panel filed back out, returning to the jury room. After twelve hours of deliberation, at 10:30 p.m. Friday night, the jury reached a verdict.

Pearl was not in the courtroom. She had collapsed that afternoon, fainted dead away while talking to Mr. and Mrs. Arnold, and was kept out of the courtroom for the reading of the verdict.

"Mr. Foreman, has the jury reached a verdict?" Judge Thompson asked.

"It has, your honor," said Bertram Wilson, the jury's foreman. "We find the defendant guilty of murder in the first degree."

"Thank you for your service," the judge said. "The jury is dismissed. Mr. Odell, I sentence you to die in the electric chair during the week of June 13th."

Observers, of course, looked to the defendant. His face had turned "chalk white." Mrs. Arnold stood briefly, and then fainted. Others rushed to her aid.

Odell turned to look back at his stepmother, and his only reaction was a single heave of his chest.

Shaffer rose to his feet and said, "I wish to make a motion to set aside the verdict as being contrary to the insufficiency of the evidence."

"Denied," the judge snapped.

Odell was then led on shaky legs to the court stenographer where he had to, for reasons unknown, answer questions regarding his age, address, marital status, education, etc. He was then led away by deputies. He gave his stepmother one last wistful glance, corrected his posture to stand erect, chin up, shoulders back, and left the courtroom. Later that night a reporter managed to see Odell and ask for a comment regarding his conviction and sentencing.

"Until they strap me down in the electric chair I'll swear I never intended to kill Kneip," Odell said.

Shaffer and Love got within a few feet of one another but did not shake hands.

"Sorry, I can't congratulate you," Shaffer said.

"I didn't expect it," Love replied.

A man with a megaphone informed the crowd outside the courthouse, which had doubled in size since the Friday night theaters let out, of the verdict and asked them to disperse—"there's no more to see, it's all over, go home"—which they did slowly.

One lady yelled out, referring to Pearl, "Give her to us! We'll give her what she deserves!"

Perhaps the guy most distressed by the near riot conditions outside the Monroe County courthouse during and following Odell's trial was Louis Fuller, Pearl's lawyer. He didn't want her trial to take place during that kind of chaos, which had to be prejudicial to a jury. He let it be known as soon as the street out in front of the court was cleared that he wanted Pearl to be tried somewhere else, anywhere—Syracuse, Buffalo, Auburn—where it could proceed under halfway normal conditions. Auburn became the early favorite as a new location because Judge Thompson had jurisdiction there and would not have to give up the case.

Odell spent the weekend in the Monroe County jail. He made up his will, in which he left "everything" to Pearl. It didn't amount to much. He was only twenty-two, after all. There was just his bankbook, a few pieces of jewelry, and the furniture in his room at the Arnold house. He didn't say so, but observers sensed he was confident that Pearl would not be punished as severely as he.

Odell was allowed to see Pearl and the two shared what was to be their last embrace for a long time. They cried bitterly on each other's shoulders until deputies pulled them apart.

"You see how things came out, Pearl," Odell said as he was pulled away. "And it was all for you."

"I'll stick with you, Jimmy. I'll stick," she said.

"I'm awful sorry I'm going away. You turn straight, be straight, tell the truth. Give the child to the folks, they'll keep it."

On Monday, Odell was taken on a tour of the sheriff's department and shook hands with the men. He had a smile for each of them and they, to a man, expressed their sympathy. Their feeling was that more justice had been dished out near Black Creek than would be done in Sing Sing's Ol' Sparky. He arranged for a present to be sent to his wife after he left. Significantly, it was a box of chocolates.

That evening, Odell took the New York Central night train to Ossining, New York, to take up his new residence in the Sing Sing death house. Accompanying him were Undersheriff William Stallknecht and Deputy Sidney O'Brien. Odell was handcuffed to O'Brien throughout the trip. There was a small group of people, maybe thirty-five, at the train station to see him, but nothing like the gathering at the courthouse.

By May 13, Pearl's attorney had given up the idea of a change of venue, convinced now that the trial was going to be a madhouse wherever it was conducted.

Fuller said that he would not be calling Odell as a witness in favor of his wife, but the prosecution did not rule out the possibility that they might call him to testify against Pearl.

Fuller's other move during the build-up to Pearl's trial was to have her examined by Dr. Max Morris to verify that she was actually pregnant—she was. Her announcement while on the witness stand had caught most everyone by surprise and Fuller wanted to verify that it wasn't another of Pearl's games.

On May 25, Judge Thompson announced that, after consulting with the sheriff, he was going to do his best to keep Pearl's trial from being the circus that her husband's trial had turned into. "Outsiders" were not only to be barred from the courtroom but from the corridors outside the courtroom as well. Folks who had business in the courthouse would be allowed in, but they could not linger in the halls.

It was noted that, despite the restriction on "outsiders," the trial would still be held before a full courtroom, as journalists from around the country had written and arranged for seating.

The press made note of the fact that this was Fuller's tenth capital punishment case and not one of his clients had gone to the electric chair.

Extra time was being allotted for jury selection, as now more than ever it was thought to be difficult to find twelve men who hadn't already made up their mind about Pearl. But, as it turned out, no extra time was necessary, and the jury box was filled in one day.

Both sides accepted jurors who had heard about the case, as long as they had not formed an opinion as to Pearl's guilt or innocence. Among those rejected were a man who had worked with Kneip and a man who knew Jimmy Odell. In the next morning's paper, all twelve jurors had their names, addresses, and occupations printed.

Some well-known men were in the jury pool, such as Herbert Weet, the superintendent of schools, but they all seemed to know how to avoid service, telling Mr. Love that they didn't believe in the death penalty.

The chosen were middle class. Judge Thompson, along with the usual instructions to not discuss the case, told the panel that he wanted to be over and done with this trial as soon as possible and planned to work through the weekend and Memorial Day.

A careful listen to the *voir dire* led observers to believe that Fuller was planning to argue that the killing of Kneip was justifiable homicide. Mr. Love's questions seemed to weed out potential jurors who would have trouble judging poorly upon a woman, especially a pregnant woman.

Warned to keep away, Rochesterians for the most part obeyed. Only about a dozen people were assembled outside the courthouse in hopes of getting a glimpse of Pearl as she came and went.

The day of jury selection is usually a boring affair and doesn't attract spectators. Pearl kept her face composed during *voir dire,* and all attorneys seemed pleased with the efficiency with which the jury box was filled.

She was slightly heavier than at her last public appearance, and one observer said she had a "noticeable pallor." Her jailers noted that Pearl had been a "light-hearted girl" until her husband was sentenced to die. Since then she had been "downcast."

Opening statements began on Thursday morning, May 27. Odell was allowed to leave Sing Sing to attend the trial. He seemed depressed throughout and there was surprisingly little interaction between the Odells.

Love told the jury that Pearl and her husband plotted out the murder of Kneip.

"Therefore, I ask for a conviction of murder in the first degree," Love said.

The trial ran along the same lines as the first one. The prosecution began with the testimony of the sheriff, sheriff's investigators, railroad personnel, and a morgue attendant describing the discovery and post-mortem examination of Kneip's body, and the crime scene. Again testifying were the witnesses who'd seen Odell and Pearl walking south on Scottsville Road near the air field days before the murder, circumstantially establishing premeditation by showing that the young couple were scouting for a location to commit their murder. Jerome Names corroborated that the Odells were out walking around West Chili days before the murder. On cross-examination Names admitted that the couple he saw was bundled up against the cold, but refused to say that this impeded his ability to recognize them. Fuller accused Names of "going off half-cocked with his answers" which brought a strong objection from Love that the judge sustained.

Next witnesses were called to establish that Odell had been trying to locate Kneip and once located, bought a pair of handcuffs on Front Street in the city and impersonated a sheriff's deputy to kidnap the victim. The cab driver that took the couple and their victim to Mosquito Point Road told his story. Testimony followed establishing that Pearl's bloody clothing had been found in the home of Odell's stepparents.

The last witness of the first day was the county stenographer who testified to transcribing Pearl Odell's confession to District Attorney Love.

The Friday morning session began with the stenographer reading Pearl's confession aloud to the jury. While many had heard the confession before, her description of Kneip's drugging her, taking her virginity on a couch, and leaving her damaged goods still packed a punch for a 1920 audience. The description of the sudden brutal violence on the night of the murder was doubly shocking. Following the reading, the prosecution rested its case.

The judge did not hold to his threat of working through the holiday weekend and instead adjourned court until the following Tuesday. The idea seemed like a good one at first, until the day came and the weather was blistering hot.

Fans inside the courtroom served only to sluggishly move the hot air around so it was a somewhat wilted and shiny Pearl who took the witness stand to tell the story of her life and the murder.

She wept on several occasions during her testimony, the first tears coming when she told of her father, when she was fourteen years old, losing his arm in a mining accident. Because he could not work, she was forced to leave the home and find work on her own. She described how Kneip had "betrayed" her and how she had demanded that he do right by marrying her.

"Were you ever in love with Mr. Kneip?" Fuller asked.

"No, sir," she replied.

She said that he, at first, promised to marry her, but the date kept being pushed back.

"He asked me to do unnatural things and he said he was out with other girls. He struck me in the face before I broke it off with him," she said with a sniffle.

She described meeting and falling in love with Odell and, for the first time, said that he too had been abusive.

"Once, when I was in bed, Jimmy shoved his knees into my stomach and held my wrists. He called me his second-hand wife."

She said that Odell became obsessed with Kneip, and that liquor made him crazy. She said that she and Odell went to see Evelyn Nesbitt in the theater one time and her husband brought up Kneip during the performance. (Evelyn Nesbitt, one of the world's first pin-up girls and supermodel, was perhaps most famous as being one corner of a love triangle that resulted in a high-profile murder in New York City. On June 25, 1906, her husband, multimillionaire Harry Thaw shot and killed her boyfriend, prominent architect Stanford White, in front of hundreds of witnesses in the rooftop theater of Madison Square Garden, back in the days when MSG was actually on Madison Square and had a garden.)

Fuller was establishing for the jury a scenario that had not come up during the first trial: that Pearl was afraid of Odell and would have gone along with anything he said out of fear.

As Pearl's testimony went on, Fuller's questions became few and far between, and her answers grew steadily longer. She sometimes drifted off the subject and Fuller had to interrupt to get her back on track. She gave an accounting of her movements at the time she and Odell were supposed to be walking Scottsville Road near Britton Field scouting locations.

Finally, she got around to the abduction, the trip to the country, and the murder. She said that, after she struck Kneip in the head for the first time with the file, he had used loutish terms to call her an insalubrious strumpet.

She did not account for the severity of Kneip's wounds.

She said he was released from the tree and fell to the ground still, but when Odell went to check on him he leaped up and the two men grappled. Kneip was getting the better of it and was choking Odell to death when she fetched a log and hit Kneip over the head with it.

"I pulled James out from under Kneip," she said. "It was nearly two minutes before Jimmy could talk. I had twisted my ankle when my shoe broke."

"How did you get home?"

"I don't remember."

"When you struck Kneip that final blow did you think Jimmy was in danger?"

"I certainly did."

"Did you at any time have any desire to kill that man?"

"No, I did not."

"How did Kneip's clothes get removed?"

"Jimmy did that."

"Did you tell Mr. and Mrs. Arnold what had happened when you got home?"

"I told Mrs. Arnold. I told her shortly after we got to the house."

"No further questions."

Judge Thompson looked to Mr. Love, who rose slowly. Asking questions in a quiet voice, Love induced Pearl to admit that she had told the story of her so-called rape several times in formal interviews before she first mentioned the drugged chocolates.

Following Pearl's testimony, Fuller put a series of witnesses on the stand to further soil Odell's character, specifically that he was a bad drinker, had a bad temper, became obsessed with things, and held grudges.

(The defense wanted to present witnesses to testify to other Odell "peculiarities" but the judge declared the evidence inadmissible. The witnesses were bosses who had fired Odell, acquaintances who'd been on the wrong end of a knuckle sandwich, and military friends who had teased Odell about something that was never made public.)

On the other hand, Pearl was presented as a woman who had been pregnant at the time of the murder, and pregnancy was known to make some women behave in an erratic manner.

It was expected that Fuller's defense would rest but Fuller asked for a little time. He explained to the court that he'd heard a rumor, he didn't want to say what it was, but it concerned potential new evidence. As this was a capital case, Judge Thompson wanted to give the defense all the leeway possible and adjourned court for the day.

Outside, a reporter asked prosecutor Love a hypothetical question: "If Pearl gets the chair, will she be allowed to have her baby?"

"Better she is executed before she gives birth," Love said. "No child should be born under such circumstances."

The district attorney had just called for the execution of an unborn child and his comment yielded nary a ripple of controversy.

When court resumed there was no further mention of the "rumor." The defense rested, and the final arguments commenced.

Fuller's oratory was scorching. He tore into Mr. Love, he insulted the members of the press, he insulted the detectives who had handled the murder back in January.

He said that one of the witnesses was a saloonkeeper who was more concerned about the Volstead Act than he was about the case at hand.

Fuller systematically went through all of the prosecution's witnesses and called them perjurers and liars. He screamed that because of decisions made by the court he was unable to "introduce into the case the necessary psychological atmosphere" to make the jury understand.

"My case would have benefitted from the French rule of evidence which permits everything pertaining to the crime,"

Fuller said.

Judge Thompson glared at him.

The jury seemed uncomfortable. While everyone else was squirming, Pearl wept quietly, obviously sensing that it wasn't going well. Cynics however claimed there were no real tears coming from the defendant's eyes.

Fuller switched his tact. He said, "The Lord said an eye for an eye and a tooth for a tooth, not two eyes for an eye and two teeth for a tooth. Pearl's husband has already been punished for this crime."

He concluded by talking about how pathetic Pearl was, motherless since age four, on her own since fourteen.

"Has she ever had a chance?" he asked the jury.

Now it was Love's turn. He reminded the jurors that they had a sworn duty to be guided by the facts, not by their emotions, and the fact in this case were clear: "This woman confederated with her husband to bring about the death of Kneip."

He described the horrible state of the body, the fact that the scalp and ears were torn to shreds and hanging on by a thread because of the defendant's use of the file.

"The defendant was *busy* around that tree," Love said. "Remember your oath. Pregnancy should not enter into this case. The only justice is to convict this woman."

The crowd control measures that had for the most part worked during Pearl's trial proved inadequate once the jury began deliberating at 4:00 p.m. on Thursday, June 3.

Crowds flocked to the courthouse in hopes that they could, through some miracle, be the first to learn Pearl's fate. The crowd was estimated at being more than a thousand people and none of them had the slightest clue what was going on inside the building.

Cars trying to navigate Main Street had to take turns passing the courthouse on the north side of the street. Some of the spectator wannabes, with knowledge of the inside layout, circled around to the Fitzhugh Street side of the building in a vain attempt to look into the jury room.

At 11:40 p.m., after seven and half hours of deliberation, the jury came to a decision. The crowd tried to rush the guards and get into the building, but to no avail.

In the courtroom, jury foreman Alfred Swan, vice-president of the Rochester Stamping Company, stood and in a shaky voice announced that they had found Pearl Beaver Odell guilty of murder in the second degree. They had decided that Pearl had not intended to kill Kneip until the attack started, but once it started she couldn't stop.

As was the custom back then, Judge Thompson sentenced Pearl right there on the spot without a separate hearing. He sentenced Pearl to twenty years in prison, with the possibility of parole after sixteen.

When she heard the verdict and sentence, Pearl broke down and cried, and by all accounts she cried for the next three days. One observer said that she'd cried more in the days following her conviction that she had in the six months prior.

The conviction had come as a surprise to her. She had fully expected to walk. A pregnant woman, taking out the man who wronged her? If that wasn't justifiable homicide, what was?

It didn't occur to her that it was her own viciousness that did her in.

Fuller told reporters that he planned to appeal the conviction, but when asked on what grounds he seemed flummoxed.

"Oh, on general grounds," he finally said.

"Will you appeal on the grounds of judicial error, saying that Judge Thompson should have allowed in all evidence that Odell was unbalanced?" the reporter inquired, obviously thinking more clearly at that moment than the defense attorney.

"Yes, yes, I think I will," Fuller said.

Some of the jurors made themselves available to the press, and it turned out that Pearl had escaped the electric chair by the skin of her teeth. The first vote included eight ayes for murder one. It wasn't until the ninth ballot that the jury agreed on murder two.

On June 7, rumors flew that Pearl had attempted suicide. The rumor started when an ambulance pulled up in front of the county jail and took away a female prisoner on a stretcher. It turned out that Pearl was fine and the woman on the stretcher was Josephine Ferone, an emaciated homeless woman arrested for vagrancy who'd been taken ill.

The next day Pearl was taken, first by car, then train, from the Monroe County Jail to Auburn prison. As Pearl left the jail, a newspaper photographer stepped forward and, far more polite than one would expect today, asked Pearl if it were ok for him to take her photo.

Pearl reportedly replied, "No, sir. If you try to take my picture I will put my hands up before my face. I will not stand for it."

At the train station she was not handcuffed, and no one recognized her as she walked with her guards to the platform and boarded the Syracuse train. She got off at the Byron stop and transferred to a train that took her to the Auburn prison.

On September 13, Pearl was rushed to Mercy Hospital where she gave birth to a healthy baby girl, who was named Mildred Naomi Odell. The law said that legally Pearl could keep the baby girl with her until she was two, at which time she had to be put up for adoption. Pearl returned to the prison, her baby in her arms, five days later.

In February 1921, Odell's appeals lawyer Hampton H. Halsey argued before the appellate court that Odell should not be executed as there was zero evidence that the murder was pre-meditated. On March 8, the court affirmed Odell's conviction. A new date for Odell's death was scheduled for April 25.

On March 17, Odell wrote a letter to his Monroe County jurors in which he said, "I am not saying what the world owes me, or the happiness I deserve, but I do claim the right, as every other man does, to be met half way, and all I can say now is I hope this great misfortune will help men and women in similar cases to place a higher value on a woman's soul. I honestly hope you will never have the heart-ache and suffering that has come to me."

At the end of March, Halsey moved for a new trial and Odell was given a new sanity test, which he passed. Halsey promised new evidence, which turned out to be a new deposition from Pearl stating that she administered the fatal blow to save her husband's life.

In April, Dr. John Steele, a representative of the Presbyterian Board of Temperance and Moral Welfare, went to Auburn and visited Pearl. Afterwards he told the press, "Mrs. Pearl Odell is not the sort of woman to have the care of her child. I think that in the interest of society it would be best to have the child trained in a home."

On April 22, 1921, Judge Adolph J. Rodenbeck denied the motion to give Odell a new trial. The judge said the evidence was clear. Odell planned the murder, and carried it out.

A last plea to New York State Governor Miller to spare Odell's life was unsuccessful. Odell wrote a letter to Pearl wishing her the best and asked her to take good care of their daughter.

Mrs. Arnold visited her stepson one last time. She was his last visitor.

Guards asked Odell what he wanted for his last meal.

"Just bring my regular dinner. I don't care for much to eat," Odell said.

At five minutes to midnight, April 27, 1921, guards came and told Odell it was time.

"Good-bye, boys!" Odell said to the twenty-two other condemned men in the death house as he took the dead-man walk.

"Good-bye, Jimmy!" they called back in unison.

Accompanying Odell down that long hallway was Dr. Rev. Anthony N. Peterson, prison chaplain. Details regarding the execution and funeral arrangements were kept secret at first.

Only after he was in the ground was news released that he'd been laid out at Michael J. Emma's funeral home on North Clinton Avenue and buried in Riverside Cemetery with only a handful of relatives in attendance. Rev. Waldo Cherry, minister of the Central Presbyterian Church officiated at the graveside services.

Ol' Sparky, the electric chair at Sing Sing.

Pearl's daughter was not immediately taken away from her as some had wanted, and there was even a birthday party in the prison when Mildred turned one. At the party a fellow inmate asked Pearl what she was going to do when she got out. Pearl said she planned to return to Rochester and "live down" her past.

On Mildred's second birthday, there was no party. Instead, as per the law, the child was taken from Pearl. It was originally reported that the child had gone to live with the

Arnolds, but Odell's stepparents denied this, saying the baby had gone to live with a "respectable family" that lived somewhere near Rochester.

A wild rumor made the front pages in 1929 when it was erroneously reported that little Mildred had actually been adopted by baseball legend George Herman "Babe" Ruth and his first wife. Mrs. Ruth had just died in a house fire, and had bequeathed $50,000 to the child—at which point the Arnold's claimed that the child was Pearl's. Mrs. Ruth had been long estranged from the Babe, and the original identity of her adopted daughter had never been made public. After a couple days of mad fuss, the story was branded absurd and went away. (The little girl in question turned out to be Ruth's by a previous outside-marriage situation.)

Franklin Delano Roosevelt

Pearl ended up serving ten years for her crime. During most of that time she received fifty cents a day working as a nurse in the prison hospital. She was released in December of 1930 after New York State Governor Franklin Delano Roosevelt commuted her sentence.

She told a reporter she would not keep her plans to return to Rochester but instead would take the train in the other direction. She had a nursing job lined up, she boasted.

"The woman who was raising my daughter recently died," she said with a euphoric smile. "So there's a chance I'll get my Mildred back. Today is one of the happiest days of my life. I am going to see my child again and I am anxious to make good and hope nothing turns up to hinder my plan..."

The reporter closed his tiny notebook, turned on a heel and left.

Pearl was alone now, but her survival instincts were intact. Her head was again filled with light-hearted dreams as she boarded a train bound for New York City.

That's David Harmon on the top right, and me on the bottom left. We were ten years old. The team photo for the Chili Senators was taken as we looked into a setting sun.

DEATH OF A FIRST BASEMAN

During the summers of 1966 and '67, I played for the Chili Senators in the tee-shirt Chili Youth Baseball league. My dad was the manager, and our first baseman was a tall kid named Dave Harmon.

We lived near the eastern edge of the town of Chili, in the Wheatland-Chili Central School district. Only a handful of W-C kids played in the league, so most of our teammates and opponents went to Gates-Chili or Churchville-Chili.

Because of that, after little league, I lost touch with Dave, but remembered him as a good kid with an excellent glove, who saved me more than a few errors by scooping my throws from second base out of the dirt.

I didn't hear about Dave in any context until 1982, fifteen years later, when my mom called and asked if I remembered him.

I said, "Sure, why?"

"He's been murdered," she said.

These were the days long before the Internet, so my mom clipped out the article in the D&C *about the murder and mailed it to me. The article said that Dave was the son of John and Susan Harmon who lived on Jensen Drive, off of Chestnut Ridge Road in the suburban Chili Center section of town.*

John was an elementary school teacher in the Gates-Chili school district.

Dave graduated from Gates-Chili in 1975, attended Olivet Nazarene College in Kankakee, Illinois south of Chicago, and in 1977, barely twenty years old, was married to his Midwestern fiancée, the former Melinda Lambert, at the Grace Church of the Nazarene in North Chili.

The article didn't give many details regarding the murder itself. Dave died of massive head injuries inflicted with a blunt object during a home invasion.

For years that was all I knew. Later my interest was rekindled…

David Harmon and Melinda Lambert met through their church. She had a father who was powerful in the church and, whether consciously or not, she went about life as if she had a safety net. Nothing too bad could ever happen to her. Her dad had her back. She was attractive, but sometimes lacked diligence; had an effervescent personality, with those bubbles sometimes rising all the way to her head. She was quick to giggle, and—when she turned to flash a flirtaceous glance—her perky bosom cut the air. Melinda liked Dave because he was tall.

Dave and Melinda moved to Olathe, Kansas, where Dave took a job with the Olathe State Bank.[3] At that job, it became clear that he had not fully reached emotional maturity, and

[3] If that name—*O-LAY-thuh*—sounds familiar, it may be because the town played a major role in the horrific true-crime story that spawned Truman Capote's *In Cold Blood*.

still enjoyed the same games and jokes that kept him amused as a kid. Not everyone might have appreciated it, for example, when he snapped rubber bands at his co-workers as they were working.

After a year, he left that job and took another at the Patrons Bank and Trust Company as a teller. He worked part-time at the bank while attending the University of Kansas, which was thirty miles from his home in the town of Lawrence.

He graduated in 1979 with a business degree, and six months after graduation was promoted to bank officer. A subsequent promotion made him assistant operations manager.

He was described by co-workers as jovial and athletic. He was active in the College Church of the Nazarene in Olathe and was president of the Sunday School there, leading about one-hundred students.

Melinda and Dave: Just kids

During the last months of his life he lost control of his appetite, ate gluttonously, a lot of fast food, and put on a great deal of weight. He made jokes about it. His broadening hips made him a better hockey goalie, he said.

His wife was secretary to the dean of students at Mid-American Nazarene College in Olathe. Olathe today is a hustling and bustling suburb, but back then it was a sleepy town, and the Christian college was its focal point and primary employer.

At about 2:30 a.m. on February 28, 1982, the Harmons' next-door neighbor Gail Bergstrand heard thumping noises on the other side of her bedroom wall, coming from the adjacent duplex apartment. By the time she woke up her husband, the disturbing sounds had stopped.

Gail couldn't get back to sleep. Those sounds, there was something sinister about them—as if someone were beating a side of beef with a baseball bat. Nothing you wanted to hear in the middle of the night. There were seven thwacks, a pause, and then seven more.

About an hour and a half later, there came loud knocking on the Bergstrand's front door. Gail knew instinctively that the knocking and the thwacking noises were connected. At the door was Melinda Harmon. She had a bruise on her cheek, and seemed on autopilot, in shock maybe, as she told them she and her husband had been attacked.

The Bergstrands called the police. When cops arrived, Melinda told them that "a couple of black guys" had broken into their duplex apartment and assaulted her and her husband.

She said that she and Dave were asleep when she was awoken at 2:20 a.m. by the sound of her husband being attacked. The two men had entered the house downstairs through the sliding glass doors in the back, which she had carelessly forgotten to lock. The men demanded keys to the Patrons Bank. She gave the men the keys and was taken downstairs.

"I overheard one guy say to the other, 'I think I hit him too hard. I think I might have killed him,'" Melinda told the police. One man then, she said, struck her in the face and knocked her unconscious. When she came to, more than an hour later, she ran next door to call police.

"All right," the first responders said. "Let's go next door and see."

They found Dave in bed, dead. Their first thought upon seeing Dave's body was that he had been shot in the face with a shotgun. It was the most brutal crime scene these policemen had ever seen. Upon closer examination, they could see he had been beaten in overkill fashion in the face and head with a round, hard object. When Gail imagined a baseball bat hitting a side of beef she had been very close to accurate.

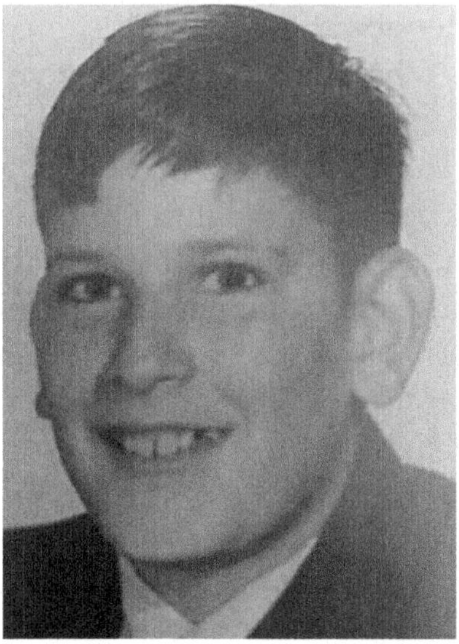

Dave, looking just like I remember him.

The scene communicated deep anger. It must be exhausting to beat a man's head into pulp like that. From the position of the body, police figured Dave never saw it coming. He'd been attacked in his sleep. His brain matter was splattered across his bedroom wall. He had been struck in the face between twelve and fourteen times—seven and seven just as Gail next door had heard it. One of his eyeballs had been knocked from its socket and was found on the rug several feet from the bed.

The weapon was not found.

Melinda was treated at the scene for minor injuries by an

Emergency Medical Technician (EMT) who didn't believe a word she said. The EMT had seen injuries that caused a person to lose consciousness. There was tremendous swelling. Expected symptoms would include bleeding on the brain, partial amnesia, loss of balance. In the great majority of cases when someone is "knocked cold" they stay out only for a minute or two. A blow that would render someone unconscious for over an hour would be traumatic. This woman had a bruise on her cheek that didn't seem serious at all. Also, revealingly, she was up and about, talking and functioning without any of the typical signs of a concussion. She claimed to have been in bed beside Dave when the attack began, yet she had no blood on her face or head. The only blood was on the bottom of her nightgown, indicating she had been standing a safe distance away when the splatter began. Her pillow, on the other hand, was well-splattered with blood and brain matter.

Although the bank keys had been taken from the scene, police did not want to speculate on the motive for the attacks. Dave was one of about twenty bank officers who had the same keys, many of whom were older and smaller and in theory a softer target for an attack. Besides, the keys were to the outer door to the bank. They wouldn't have helped anyone get into the vault where the money was.

While crime-scene investigators were still going over the apartment looking for clues, Melinda called a friend, Mark Mangelsdorf, a six-foot-four student at the college, to come over and give her emotional support. Mark arrived promptly, looking freshly showered, his hair wet, and gave Melinda a broad shoulder to cry on.

Police staked out the bank but no robbers showed up. In light of the theft, however, all of the locks at the bank were changed.

In charge of the homicide investigation was Detective Vernon Wilson of the Metropolitan Major Case Investigation

Squad. He had many questions.

"Why would someone steal the keys to a bank on a Sunday morning?" Wilson wondered out loud. "Still, there is nothing in Harmon's background that would indicate that someone would want to kill him. The missing keys are the only possible motive we've got. But it just doesn't figure. It doesn't seem right."

Within forty-eight hours of the murder, Wilson said that they had suspects in the case and were awaiting the results of tests before issuing warrants for their arrests. Area banks were offering a total of $10,000 in reward money for information leading to an arrest. But there was no arrest.

Detective Wilson dropped the "bank keys" angle completely and focused his investigation on Melinda's relationship with Mark Mangelsdorf, a male student at MidAmerican Nazarene College where she worked at the time of Dave's death, the very same Mark Mangelsdorf whom she'd called for emotional support on the night of the murder. He lived only a few blocks away from the Harmons, and the guy couldn't account for his whereabouts at the time of the murder. Being tall, Mark was Melinda's type.

David Harmon as an adult.

Shortly after the murder, a pair of K9 teams had been brought in to help the investigation. Both dogs, one at a time, sniffed from the Harmon's duplex apartment to a trash receptacle next to Mark's apartment. Nothing incriminating was found in that trash, but the fact that the dogs went from one abode to the other was considered significant.

Police had asked Mark if they could look around his apartment.

"Sure," he said.

Inside the front door were spots of blood on the floor, but with the primitive forensic technology available to police in those days, there was no way to connect the blood with David Harmon.

In Mangelsdorf's clothes hamper, investigators found a pair of soiled underwear.

"Poop your pants, Mark?" they asked.

"Uh, yeah. I had a stomach ache yesterday. I was supposed to play hockey with Dave but had to stay home."

Investigators asked around and learned that Mark Mangelsdorf was a college superstar who was expected to go far in life. The Harmons and Mangelsdorf had been quite the threesome. Mark was good friends with both Dave and Melinda, witnesses said. Sometimes it was weird because Mark's car would be in the Harmons' driveway even though Dave's wasn't there.

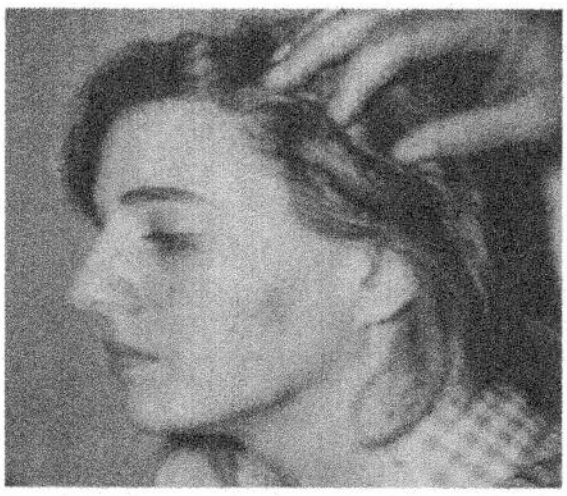

Melinda shows a police photographer the bruise on her cheek.

The biggest complicating factor in the investigation was Melinda's dad, J. Wilmer Lambert, who was a bigwig in Olathe, an upper echelon official in *the* church. He had a lot of elected officials in his hip pocket. You couldn't get elected in Olathe without the church's approval, and Lambert had a lot to say about who did and didn't get approved.

It appeared to Detective Wilson that Melinda's dad was doing his best to keep the investigation from following its natural course. Lambert screamed bloody murder every time someone tried to interview his daughter, who continued to tell a story that didn't make much sense.

The question was simple: Why was the attack on David so vicious and the attack on her so mild? His head was turned to pulp; she had a small bruise on her face.

But Lambert hurled threats and insults whenever the police approached the truth, and he eventually got his way.

One exchange typified the cops' frustration. Police picked up Melinda and tried to take her to police headquarters to be read her rights before she was to be "questioned closely."

The old man intercepted the pick-up.

"Mr. Lambert, she is going with us and she will be questioned," Detective Wilson said.

"The hell she will," her dad said. "She's coming home with me right now, you bumbling pieces of shit."

He grabbed her by the shirt and roughly pulled her away from the police. In a lot of places that would have earned Lambert an obstruction of justice charge, but not in Olathe where authorities made no further attempt to talk to Melinda.

At Dave's funeral, Melinda and Mark sat next to one another in the front of the church. She at one point put her head on Mark's shoulder, oblivious to the fact that all eyes were on them. Mark responded by whispering something in her ear.

Dave's parents went to Olathe and were at Dave's funeral there. They remembered it being a strange and haunting day.

Something was very wrong.

Mom Sue said, "David was a kind, outgoing, and meticulous man who seemed to be very much in love with his wife. He and Melinda had a normal courtship. She was anxious to get married. Her relatives all agreed because David was a fine young man—a good catch. We liked her, but we thought they were too young to be married. They were in their teens when they met at a church camp in New York State. They were barely in their twenties when they married."

John added, "Our daughter-in-law acted strangely after David's death. We reached out to her at the funeral. We wanted to talk to her, but we were *not allowed* to be in the room with her alone. Her relatives and her friends were with her all the time."

Sue said, "She ignored us. It wasn't natural. We haven't seen or heard from her since the funeral. We knew the case was still active, especially during the last couple of years. Investigators came to our home looking for anything that might help close the case."

John said, "There were a lot of questions about the veracity of her story. Why would intruders kill one person and leave another witness alive? It didn't hold water."

David Harmon was buried in Oak Lawn Cemetery in Olathe.

As for Mark Mangelsdorf, he and Melinda didn't see each other very much after the murder. With Dave gone, folks figured, their relationship became too awkward and was discontinued.

In 1983, Melinda moved to Ohio to be close to her family. She graduated from Ohio State University. In 1984 she began dating a dentist named Dr. Mark Raisch. In 1986 they were married, had two children, and she took a job working in his office. The couple lived in an upper-class community about fifteen miles north of Columbus, where the houses were large and far apart, set upon large landscaped lots.

Melinda became known as an assertive person with the ability to get things done. For example, she once organized opposition to a new road that was to be built, protesting on the grounds that it would eat up much needed green space in her neighborhood.

In 2001, the Olathe police still felt the sting of the murder investigation that was usurped almost twenty years early. Detective Bill Wall gave the case a fresh look. He decided to drop in unexpectedly on Melinda and Mark, wherever they might be, and see how they reacted to questions that should have been asked long before.

Wall had a reputation as a guy whose interrogations ended in confessions. He didn't use physical force, but rather keen psychological techniques.

First stop was Melinda Raisch's home outside Columbus, Ohio. Detective Wall, along with two other officers, rang her doorbell. She was home alone, and answered the door wearing only a bathrobe.

"Hi, Melinda. I'm with the Olathe Police Department. We came to talk to you about the murder of your husband, David. We've re-opened the case and we're hoping you can help us."

"Sure, come on in," she said. "Care for coffee? I'll make a fresh pot."

They said no thanks to the coffee and, after Melinda put on clothes, they sat around the kitchen table.

"First off," Wall said. "You were there that night. Tell us what you remember about David's murder."

"Well," Melinda said, "I remember that night seeing a man, a shadowy figure hitting David. I ran to the bathroom and then downstairs. And the man came down. And it was dark. He was in the living room. He was wearing a homemade cloth mask."

"You seem to be remembering it differently," Wall said. The two black men were gone and a man wearing a cloth mask had taken their place. "Did you lie back then?"

"I didn't lie," Melinda insisted. "But I have a feeling, a feeling in my heart"—she held her hands to her chest—"that this is how it happened."

Wall lied and told Melinda they had made excellent use of the new DNA technology.

"We know that it had to be you or Mark who killed David," Wall said.

"Well, I can tell you this. I did not kill my husband. Let me get that clear right now," Melinda replied. "When I saw the shadowy figure of the man in the cloth mask I knew in my heart that it was Mark."

"Why would Mark want to kill Dave?"

"Well…"

"Did you and Mark have a relationship?"

"We had an inappropriate relationship, but nothing physical. Mark had feelings for me."

It was at that point that Melinda realized she needed a lawyer and she discontinued the interview. Detective Wall was exhilarated by his success.

One down, one to go. Wall knew that getting Mark to talk was going to be much harder. He would be a tougher nut to crack. The plan was to offer Melinda a deal if she would testify against Mark, but they didn't say that out loud. Not yet.

The D.A. in Johnson County, Kansas, at that point was Paul Morrison. Although the church was still a powerful force in the community, time had built a buffer between it and Dave's murder. Mark and Melinda had moved away long ago, and a prosecution of them would no longer feel like an attack on the church itself.

The years had been kind to Mark. He had been a superstar student, getting a master's degree in marketing at Harvard Business School after leaving Olathe, and he was a superstar in business, too, climbing the corporate ladder, a future marketing CEO in the making. Now he was a senior V.P. at

Parmalat, a global consumer product company. He'd been twice married and had four kids, with another on the way. The surprise visit to his posh home—in Pelham, New York, just north of New York City—went about as anticipated.

"Hi, Mark," Detective Wall said with a big smile on his face. He introduced himself and his companions. "We are going to need a minute of your time. Anyone else here?"

Mark said no.

"We'd like you to come down to the police station here with us and share some new developments in the Dave Harmon case."

"I'd prefer to not do anything without a lawyer," Mark replied.

"We talked to Melinda," Wall said, still sounding cheerful. "Have you talked to her lately?"

"No."

"When was the last time you talked to her?"

"Olathe."

"You haven't seen her in twenty years?"

"No."

"Well, we'd still like to share some new developments with you."

"I still…still don't…"

"Did we catch you off guard here a little bit?"

"Absolutely."

"Well, the new developments have to do with DNA. We'd like to take a DNA sample from you."

"Let me call my lawyer."

"Okay," Detective Wall said. Big smile. He would wait.

Mark left and two minutes later returned. "I couldn't get in touch with him."

"We'd really like to swab you. Only takes a second."

Mark thought about that. He had hung out at Dave and Melinda's place all the time. How could his DNA get him in trouble? He opened his mouth and allowed Detective Wall to insert the long Q-Tip.

On December 5, 2003, Melinda Raisch, now forty-six years old, was indicted for the murder of David Harmon. The indictment read:

"Mark Mangelsdorf and/or Melinda Harmon aka Melinda Raisch struck David Harmon in the head with a blunt instrument, killing him. [They] moved the blanket covering the body of David Harmon, pulled out a drawer in the bedroom and took a lid off a dish containing keys to make it appear as though a residential robbery had occurred."

Mark lawyered up, hiring Mickey Sherman, to represent him. Sherman was best known as the man who unsuccessfully defended Kennedy-cousin Michael Skakel for the murder of Martha Moxley in Greenwich, Connecticut.

Days after her indictment, Melinda was arrested in Delaware County, Ohio, and charged with first-degree murder and conspiracy to commit first-degree murder.

At her court hearing she sat with downcast eyes and answered questions put to her by the judge in a hushed voice. No one from her family was there. She was released on $300,000 bond. Her lawyer, Mark Collins, said Melinda had always been a model citizen and they were opposing extradition.

Back at home in Chili, Dave's Dad John said, "We always had our suspicions."

Mom Sue added, "I just want to see closure to it. It's been open all this time and we just want to see the end of it." As for their grief, Sue concluded, "It never leaves you, the pain of losing a child."

On January 9, 2004, Melinda Raisch turned herself in and voluntarily returned to Kansas. Her arrest shocked the town of Olathe. The news was all over the television.

Detective Wall characterized Melinda for a TV news reporter as "a soccer mom living in luxury, just your perfect neighbor next door."

For that same TV report, Kevin Jakabosky, a close friend of David's, commented: "I think David kind of idolized her. I think he was really, really enamored and in love with his wife."

Newspapers called Mark a "charismatic student leader, still a teenager when they met." Melinda reportedly introduced Mark to David, who quickly accepted him, not as a romantic rival, but as a "part of the family."

Jakabosky remembered that time well: "I would pass by their house on a daily basis, and I would see Mark's car over there all the time. It seemed a little strange to me, but I kind of chalked it up as, 'Well, they've taken him under their wing.'"

With Melinda under arrest, Detective Wall felt free to talk about things that happened during the initial stages of their investigation that struck him as odd. For one thing, when police first arrived, Melinda did not seem overly concerned about her husband. When she learned he was dead, the first call she made was not to her family or church. She called Mark, who came over immediately. Even though it was the middle of the night, Mark arrived with wet hair, as if he'd just stepped out of the shower. Wall said he suspected Melinda and Mark from that first day, and both left town, separately, soon thereafter.

A preliminary hearing held in Olathe resulted in Judge James Leben holding Melinda over for trial. He ruled that Melinda's statement to Detective Wall in Ohio would be admissible at trial. Formally arraigned on the murder charges, with defense attorney Tom Bath at her side, Melinda pleaded not guilty and was freed on $300,000 bond.

Back in Pelham, Mark was trying to go about his life as if nothing were wrong. This was made more difficult by the fact that someone was writing letters to many of his friends and neighbors asking if they knew Mark was a murderer. The letter campaign got to the point where Mark hired a private detective to find out who was penning the letters. The detective hired a handwriting expert. The letters were eventually traced to a woman in Manhattan, Kansas, who had been David's friend. She agreed to stop writing the letters, but continued to call television reporters to make sure they were aware of the latest developments in the case.

At 10:00 p.m., April 4, 2005, Mark's phone rang in his Pelham home. It was a detective from the Pelham Police Department.

"Could you come outside, please?" he asked.

Mark stepped outside and was promptly grabbed and handcuffed.

"I'd like to say goodbye to my wife," Mark said.

"Sorry, you're coming with us."

Two days later, Mark appeared in a Westchester County Criminal Court where he waived his right to challenge extradition, and was taken to Olathe on a plane sent to New York specifically to bring him back. He arrived in Johnson County, Kansas, late on a Friday night, too late for a bail hearing, and spent the weekend in jail. On Monday morning he posted $300,000 bond and caught a commercial flight back to New York.

Melinda's trial began on April 11, 2005. In attendance every day to watch the proceedings was seventy-three-year-old John Harmon. He didn't take part in the trial in any way but he did talk to the press. John explained that he was there alone because David's mom had passed away the previous year. She had died of complications from heart disease and diabetes. John was convinced that the loss of their only child shortened Sue's life.

John offered a Kansas reporter a vivid picture of his son's crime scene: "David's face looked like a piece of steak. It was raw. There were blood splatters on the wall fifteen feet away."

There was an impressive gathering of press in the

courtroom, including a film crew from ABC News that was producing a segment on the murder for their *Primetime Live* TV show.

Notably absent at the trial was Melinda's father, who had done so much to derail the initial investigation. Now he was nowhere to be seen. Melinda's dentist husband, Dr. Mark Raisch, did attend every day of the trial. At the time of the trial, the Raisch's children were eleven and fifteen years old.

The nine-men, five-women jury was all white. There was no way Melinda's defense team, Tom Bath and Randy Austin, wanted African-Americans on the jury because of the racist nature of her initial story.

The prosecution was led by Johnson County District Attorney Paul Morrison, a combative and ambitious man who made it clear that if he'd been the D.A. when David Harmon was killed, justice would have been served a long time ago.

Morrison's opening statement centered on motive. Melinda Harmon wanted her husband dead for the simple reason that, because of her prominent standing in the church, she could not face the shame of divorce.

"In her *twisted* world," the D.A. said, practically spitting the words, "it was better to be a widow than to be a divorcee."

In his opening, Bath scoffed at Morrison's idea of a motive. The Harmons were deeply in love. Their marriage was strong. And besides, divorce was not the end of the world, even in Olathe. This didn't happen in 1882. It was 1982!

"Fifty-four bucks and a fifteen-minute hearing, and boom, they would have been divorced," Bath said.

Richard Bergstrand testified that, on the day before Dave's murder, he'd seen Melinda and Mark walking in a romantic strolling kind of way, even pausing at one point to kiss.

This was in sharp contrast to the statement Mark had made initially to investigators, that he was home staying close to the toilet because of an intestinal bug, an illness that caused him to miss his hockey game with Dave.

Richard's wife Gail testified about the sounds she had

heard through the wall, the thwacking that reminded her of a baseball bat hitting a side of beef. She also testified about Melinda's visit to the Bergstrand's apartment an hour and a half later, saying she had been knocked out. True, she had a small bruise on her face, but her equilibrium was excellent, she spoke clearly, and most significantly from a medical viewpoint, she remembered everything right up until the instant she was hit.

Two neurologists, Dr. Andrew Kaufman and Dr. Richard Dubinsky, testified that a blow that could knock Melinda out would have affected her memory of the minutes and perhaps hours before she received her concussion. Dubinsky added to his testimony a personal anecdote: he'd been hit by a car as a boy and didn't remember the whole day before it happened.

A police investigator testified regarding the search of Mark's apartment, and the discovery of blood on his rug and inside his vacuum cleaner. A DNA expert testified that there was a ninety-eight percent chance that the blood was David Harmon's.

A crime-scene investigator who had been at the Harmon's apartment soon after the murder testified that there was blood all over Melinda's pillow, yet none on her face and head, debunking her story that she had been asleep with her head on her pillow when the attack began.

The prosecution introduced into evidence the twenty love letters between Melinda and Mark, letters that speculated on how wonderful being together could be if David were no longer around.

The defense's key witness was Mark himself. He testified without as much as a glance at Melinda.

"I was not in love with Melinda," Mark testified at one point, sounding angry when he said it. He balled his fist and struck at the side of the wooden witness stand. The gesture was meant to emphasize his point, but came off as violent and made a sound so loud that several jurors were startled. He told the jury that David and Melinda had taken him "under their wing." And no he did *not* kill David Harmon.

On cross-examination, Bath asked Mark about the soiled underwear found in his apartment.

"I had an intestinal bug or something," Mark said.

"Is that why you didn't play hockey with David on the day before the murder?"

"Yes."

"Did your intestinal bug bother you when you went for a walk with Melinda instead? Did it bother when you stopped to kiss her?"

"I didn't think I'd ever be far from a restroom," Mark replied.

When Mark's time on the stand was through he left the courtroom and there was a scene in the hallway that struck observers as inappropriately celebratory. Mark, his wife, and his lawyers high-fived all around. They acted as if they had won something, but what?

The foreman of the trial's jury later said that he and his fellow panelists were not impressed with Mark's performance on the witness stand. They found him robotic and rehearsed.

Melinda did not testify in her own behalf, but jurors were allowed to hear tape recordings of her speaking with investigators in 2001, when she reduced the number of home invaders responsible for her husband's death from two to one and admitted changing the story she'd originally given and "knowing in her heart" that the masked man was Mark.

District Attorney Paul Morrison said in his final argument that Melinda's initial statement to authorities on the night of David's murder was the key. It was a lie. It had to be a lie because it was "implausible if not impossible" for the murder to have happened the way she said it did.

On May 3, 2005, after eleven-and-a-half hours of deliberation, the jury notified the court that they'd reached a verdict. For the reading of the verdict, Mark was not there but his team of lawyers was.

The jury found Melinda guilty of both first-degree murder

and conspiracy to commit murder. She showed little emotion but did hold a Kleenex to her nose. Up until that point, Melinda had been free on bail, but bail was now revoked and for the first time she went to jail, where she would remain until her sentencing. She was issued a striped jumpsuit and quickly became the leader of the jail's Bible-study group.

John Harmon was asked if he was going to attend Mark's trial also. He replied that he hadn't yet made up his mind, that he wanted to "sit back and take a deep breath and survey the situation a little bit."

Was he rooting for a harsh sentence for Melinda?

"I have no joy in this. I have closure. But, on the other hand, I feel very sad about her. Their family unit is torn apart. But she's responsible for her actions. As a Christian, I have freely forgiven her."

But authorities wanted Mark Mangelsdorf behind bars, and they knew that to do that, they were going to need Melinda's cooperation.

"We expect to call her as a witness in his case," said D.A. Paul Morrison.

"How will her cooperation with your prosecution affect her sentence?" a reporter asked.

Melinda Raisch. Believe it or not, this is a mug shot. She was just a happy lady.

"We expect that her cooperation will serve to lessen her jail time," Morrison replied. Of course, why else would she cooperate unless there was something in it for her?

While in jail, Melinda wrote letters and it was a letter she wrote but didn't mail that ended up getting her in trouble. She wrote that she knew at the time that Mark had purchased a crow bar a week before Dave's murder. She referred to the letter, unable to remember if she'd mailed it or not, during a monitored phone conversation. One day, while she was eating, authorities shook down her jail cell and found the letter.

Mark's luck had turned for the worse as well. Not only was the notion that he was a killer more widespread than ever because of the trial and the publicity it brought, but the company he worked for had been found to keep two sets of books, and ended up folding under an Enron-like financial scandal.

Melinda's conviction was overturned and Melinda was allowed to plead guilty to second-degree murder with the understanding that, when the time came, she would testify against Mark.

In a preliminary deposition—that is, under oath—Melinda told Morrison that Mark crept into her marital bedroom and "crushed David's skull with a crowbar."

With the case against Mark shored up, the Olathe district attorney's office tried to deal with Mark's defense attorney. Mickey Sherman was a deal-maker. They negotiated back and forth until Paul Morrison made his final offer: plead guilty to murder two, admit guilt in court, and get ten-to-twenty years, parole eligibility in five. Mark said OK.

On February 13, 2006, Mark was back in an Olathe court. Melinda's deposition was read aloud. In it, she said that Mark had been an excellent student but was inexperienced with women. Melinda was flirtaceous and bored with her marriage.

Mark and Melinda would sneak off and kiss. Mark used to open up the drawer in the night table next to Melinda's marital bed and count the condoms, keeping track of how often Melinda and Dave "did it." Conversations turned to how nice life would be if Dave disappeared. Mark talked about tampering with the brakes on Dave's car. He told her when he bought the crowbar. He told her "the time was coming." When the time did come Melinda did not warn Dave of the impending danger. She, in fact, left the back door open so Mark would be able to get in. Mark then came into the bedroom, and while Melinda stepped away to a safe distance, he hit Dave in the head again and again as hard as he could. Melinda retreated to another room and when Mark joined her she asked him if Dave was dead. He went back and gave what was left of Dave's head another thwack for good measure. They staged the robbery, then Mark hit Melinda with his fist, hard enough to leave a bruise but not so hard as to hurt her badly. He then left to clean himself up and she awaited an arranged time before reporting the "home invasion." At Dave's funeral, Mark sat down next to her in the church. She put her head on his shoulder and he whispered to her, "I got rid of the crowbar."

Following the reading of the statement, Mark pleaded guilty to intentional second-degree murder.

"I'm interested in serving the time as soon as possible so that my family and I can get on with the rest of our lives," Mark told the court. He remained free on bail until his May 2006 sentencing.

On March 27, 2006, Melinda received the plea deal she had been promised, despite the fact that her cooperation with the prosecution of Mark was now moot. Her deposition had done the trick. She pleaded guilty to second-degree murder.

"It was Melinda's agreeing to testify against Mangelsdorf that led to him pleading guilty, so we felt it appropriate to keep our end of the bargain," said D.A. Morrison, adding that Mark and Melinda were not scheduled to be sentenced together but they were scheduled to be sentenced on the same day.

That day was May 12, 2006. Mark's sentencing came first, before Judge Thomas Bornholdt. John Harmon was there to read his "impact statement" to the court and to Mark.

The aged father of my first baseman stood and spoke in a slightly shaky voice: "Mark, I met you once before when David introduced you to my wife and myself. I waited for twenty-four years to talk to you in just this setting. My comments to you are based on what I have observed. I'm drawing conclusions based on your actions and behavior. Actions have consequences. When you and Melinda conspired to commit premeditated murder, you both unleashed a chain reaction of consequences that continue to this very day. And I guess I'm very much afraid those consequences will continue into the future that will affect you and Melinda and your respective families. Your senseless act took away any chance we had for grandchildren. Mark, in some ways I do envy you. You have five children. Chances are that at some point you will be blessed with grandchildren. Do you have any idea, any remote concept of what it feels like when well-meaning friends talk about and show pictures of their grandchildren in my presence? It tears me up every day inside. In spite of what you have done I forgive you unconditionally, but I am filled with sadness for you, Mark. You've destroyed yourself. What a waste. I pray for you now. Maybe, just maybe, there still lingers in you a bit of conscience and honest reconciliation with your God. Then, once that is done, you can start on the road to restitution. I pray, Mark, I truly pray that God has mercy on your soul."

Mark was then given an opportunity to speak to John Harmon: "Mr. Harmon, I can't even begin to imagine the grief and sorrow you and your wife experienced for the loss of David. I can tell you as a father of five how much I love my children, and I know the special bond that exists between a parent and a child. So what I can say is that I'm truly, truly sorry for David's death and for the loss of time you've experienced not being able to spend time with him. There has not been a lot of time on a lot of days since 1982 that I haven't wished I could turn back the clock and do something that would change the events of that night. I thought of David on that horrible night and I wished that I could change something to bring him back—but I can't, of course. What I do know is that I have pled guilty to this. I've acknowledged my involvement and I hope in some small way that helps for you to have some closure to this. While I can't go back, and I wish I could, I can't. So, my commitment going forward is that I will in every fashion that I'm able continue to try to do what is right the best I can. And for the foreseeable future, I don't know how this will play out, but I look for those opportunities, however that exists. I am sorry. I'm very sorry."

Judge Bornholdt asked Mark why he and the victim's wife had committed the murder, what was the motive. Mark replied they did it because their religion was strict and did not condone divorce.

The judge then sentenced Mark to no less than ten years and no more than twenty years on the Kansas correctional system.

Outside the courtroom following his guilty plea, Mark told KCTV, a Kansas City television station, that his wife had just had a baby, his fifth child, so he had a lot to live for after he served his time.

Mark's wife of nine years, Kristina, told a reporter after the hearing that she fully intended to support her husband throughout his incarceration.

"We will visit him as frequently as I can," Kristina said. "We're going to stay a family and we are going to get through this."

John Harmon was again asked his reaction and gave a now familiar answer: "I do feel a sense of relief, but I feel a sense of sadness. I'm kind of relieved that it's over because it's been a long time. Our family is destroyed. I lost my son."

Melinda's sentencing hearing was held two hours later in a different courtroom but in the same courthouse, before Judge Leben. Melinda was dressed in her striped Johnson County jail jumpsuit.

The judge compared David Harmon to the hero in the classic movie *It's a Wonderful Life*. "He was a kind, giving, and talented young man, a George Bailey type. His loss and the ripple effects cannot be measured, but are quite real."

Again John Harmon was given the opportunity to address the defendant directly. "Melinda," he said, "I hold you more responsible than Mark. You, as the wife, you could have put a stop to this plot at any time—even on the night of the killing."

John read a long statement that in large part repeated what he'd earlier said to Mark. He again talked about the grandchildren he would never have.

Mark Mangelsdorf

Melinda was given the opportunity to come to the podium and speak directly to her former father-in-law—and that was when things became bizarre. With her usual happy, happy smile, Melinda took the podium. She squinted at the gallery.

"John, where are you, I can't see," she said. And she giggled, a little girl giggle, the same giggle that had made her seem so bubbly when she was a girl and a young woman, but now just betrayed a personality disorder. She was oblivious to the depth and meaning of the situation she was in. "Oh there you are," she added, with another smaller laugh.

Having located John Harmon, she immediately turned away from him, placed a piece of paper on the lecturn in front of her and read aloud to Judge Leben.

"First of all, Judge, I wish to express my deep remorse and sorrow for ever having been involved in this. I am extremely remorseful and horrified that this event occurred. I in no way intend to minimize it. If I need to be specific about my guilt to you today it is that I had knowledge about this event occurring and that I lied about it subsequently. It is a shame and remorse that I will carry with me for the rest of my life."

Then she turned back to John Harmon. "To the Harmon family, I am really, really sorry. Words do not adequately express the things I feel in my heart. Just words are not enough. I would love to have better than words. I just don't. I am very, very remorseful and would in no way ever expect any amount of time to make up for this. The life of David Harmon was an inspiration to all who knew him, including me, and I am horrified beyond words that I was connected to this. I knew the minute it happened that it was wrong, and I was scared to death and didn't know how to be strong enough to tell the truth about it. For that I am very, very sorry. I also apologize that I have not had the chance to contact Mr. Harmon all these years. I would have done so but was prevented from doing so by my attorneys, and through my year of incarceration here I have also been prevented from contacting him in any manner. So today is the first chance that I have had. I am very, very remorseful. David Harmon was an uplifting and caring person to all who knew him. They would agree on that. I consider him a fine example of how to live a life. I greatly missed him from the moment of his death, and I will always miss him for as long as I live."

The key point to be gathered from Melinda's childish

statement was that she wasn't just very remorseful, she was very, very remorseful.

It was Judge Leben's turn, and he said, "Since moving to Ohio, and especially in the period following her marriage to Dr. Raisch, the defendant has led an exemplary life. The Court surely cannot know and I do not know her motives. I can't make a finding about her motives. Perhaps she has been trying to make amends for her past crime. Perhaps she has simply regained her senses and truly possesses a strong moral character as so many of her friends attest and David Harmon once believed. I sentence you, Melinda Raisch, to ten to twenty years in prison."

Mark took a small tour of Kansas's prison system. He began his stretch in El Dorado, the newest of the state's correctional facilities situated along the Walnut River, where he was a prison mate of serial killer Dennis Rader, the infamous BTK (Bind Torture Kill). From there he was transferred to Lansing Prison, memorable to true crime fans as the spot where Dick Hickock and Perry Smith were hung at the end of Truman Capote's *In Cold Blood*.

Melinda went to the Topeka Correctional Facility, the state's only all-female prison. She was assigned minimum security status.

In 2007, Melinda Raisch was featured on an episode of *Snapped* on the Oxygen network. Former *New York Times* reporter and Sarah Lawrence College writing teacher Marek Fuchs wrote a book about the case called *A Cold-Blooded Business*.

From her prison cell, Melinda wrote John Harmon a letter of apology. Harmon by this time had re-married.

He was asked if he accepted the apology and he shrugged.

"It's hard to tell how sincere she is. She has done so much lying over the years," he said.

In 2011, both Mark and Melinda came up for parole, but

parole was denied. John Harmon was on hand to argue against Mark and Melinda's release.

The parole board, when announcing their decision, said that they didn't believe the pair had served enough time, noting that the evidence supported pre-meditated murder and the actual killing "indicated a particular ruthlessness."

In 2013, the Kansas Prisoner Review Board set Melinda's release date for April 29, 2015. Her attorney Tom Bath was asked if he had any comment about this news and he said he had not been in touch with her and had no idea what she planned to do when she got out. He was done with her.

And so, on April 29, fifty-seven-year-old Melinda Raisch walked out of prison, free on parole. She returned to Ohio.

On May 4, 2016, Mark Mangelsdorf was released. He'd served ten years.

How Mad Dog Sullivan whacked Johnny Flowers at... THE BLUE GARDENIA

Soldiers of fortune will tell you, you've got to go where the war is. The same is true for pro killers. That's why on December 17, 1981, Joseph "Mad Dog" Sullivan found himself on the New York State Thruway in his peach-colored Caddy, heading toward Rochester. The Flower City was where the war was.

Mad Dog Sullivan

Sullivan was already a legend, deadly and slippery, the only man ever to escape from Attica Prison, the guy who once escaped a jail on Governor's Island in New York Harbor by swimming across the Buttermilk Channel to Brooklyn. As a killer he was at the top of his class: thirty notches on his gun, including Westies boss Mickey Spillane.

In New York City and elsewhere, the Mob was divvied up into "families," named after the boss—or sometimes a still-respected past boss. In Rochester the warring factions didn't have names, they had letters:

—the A team, led by charismatic Salvatore "Sammy G" Gingello and Samuel "Red" Russotti, and

—the B team, ruled by Tom Didio.

Their war was called the Alphabet War. The epicenter of the conflict was an Italian restaurant on Empire Boulevard in Irondequoit called The Blue Gardenia, named after the 1953 *film noir*. The joint was part of the Empire Plaza strip mall, a well-known mob hangout where the clam sauce was *squisito*, as long as there wasn't a body in your linguine.

At 11:30 a.m. on March 2, 1978, a ten-inch galvanized steel pipe bomb was placed in a snow bank in the Gardenia's parking lot and detonated as Gingello got out of his car. He was tossed into the air by the blast but unharmed.

Six weeks later, Gingello wasn't as lucky. He was returning to his parked car across the street from Ben's Café Society in downtown Rochester when a second bomb detonated, and this time he had both legs blown off. He flipped off the cops before expiring on a gurney. Crime scene investigators later found his shoe, with his foot still in it.

Gingello was off the board. Russotti knew he was next on the list. He could've stepped down, retired to Florida, but instead fought back. In July 1978, Tom Didio was tommy gunned to death at the Exit 45 Motel in Victor.

The B team had a prolific bomb-maker and there were explosions all over the east side: Yahambas Social Club on Franklin Street, the Club of Monroe, the 1445 Club on University Avenue, the Discount Furniture Store in the Goodman Plaza. Using guns, there were unsuccessful hit attempts on B team soldiers Rosario Chirico and Rodney Starkweather, both in Greece.

As the decade came to an end the biggest damage to the B team came not from A team assassins but from the Law. Seven members of the gang were indicted on racketeering charges. Starkweather rolled over like a languid courtesan and agreed to testify against his B teammates.

The A team had won. B team was in jail and for a time all was quiet on the streets. Then Team C raised its bulbous head, led by an ambitious pair named Thomas Taylor and Thomas Torpey. Taylor had played football with Mad Dog Sullivan in Attica, and when he needed a job done, he bypassed local talent and called Sullivan, who said goodbye to his wife, and called his girlfriend, Theresa.

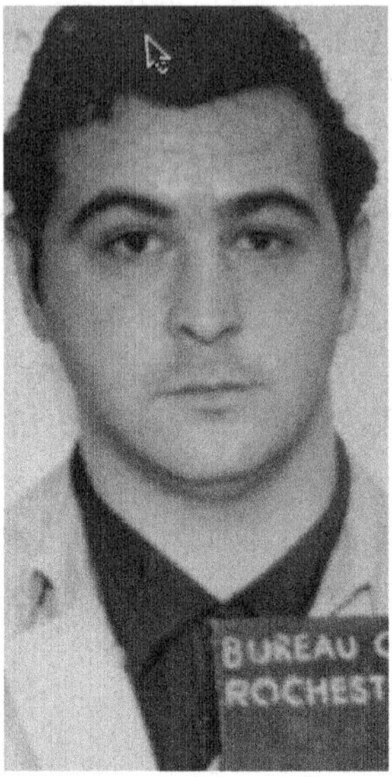

Sammy Gingello, legs blown off by a bomb, flipped off the cops before expiring on a gurney.

Joseph George "Mad Dog" Sullivan was born on March 31, 1939, in Queens, N.Y., the first-born son of a New York City cop and his wife. (He would later refer to himself using his confirmation name, Joseph John Sullivan.) Eventually, Joseph had three brothers and two sisters.

The Sullivans lived in a neighborhood called Belle Harbor, nicknamed Irish Town, which shared a long sandbar with Rockaway Beach and Breezy Point. If you lived there, you had to take a bridge or a boat to get anywhere else.

Joseph was named after his dad's brother who died at twenty-two. Uncle Joe, dead years before Joseph was born, had been a tackle on the Notre Dame Fighting Irish football team, had plans to go into the monastery, but died of pneumonia following a series of concussions on the playing field. There had been a dark cloud over Yankee Stadium that autumn when Notre Dame took on Army and ol' number 79 wasn't there.

Joseph was also the grandson of a cop. His grandfather, Big Tim Sullivan, had been an NYPD captain.

Joseph was an altar boy at St. Elizabeth's Church, where he was seduced by a nun, and sang in the choir. When he was thirteen, he and his dad were scheduled to go to a baseball game at Yankee Stadium, but his father had to cancel because he wasn't feeling well. Soon thereafter he went into the hospital and died.

Joseph moved in with his aunt and uncle so his mother could better overcome her grief. The aunt had taut downturned lips and hated all men. She cloaked her tortures, denials, and deprivations in a cowl of Catholicism, chanting the rosary like an incantation as she abused the boy.

Joseph later commented, "She had a crucifix on her wall big enough for me to nail a midget on."

He returned home to mom, and was shocked at the way things had deteriorated. His mother had built a shrine to his father in their home, turned to drink, and began to berate young Joseph. She made him kneel in front of a photograph of his father and pray that he could be half the man her husband had been. As he preyed she'd hit him in the head and say, "Don't bother. You'll never be the man he was." (Despite what must have been ambivalent feelings, Joseph later got a tattoo on his left arm that read "MOM".) She accused him of killing his father with his selfishness, which stung, even though the boy knew it couldn't be true. He'd had nothing to do with dad's death, but his mom saying it was like she was taking a whip to his back.

Within a year, he ran away. The last thing his mother said to him was, "Honey, could you get me a bottle of beer from the refrigerator?"

He was caught, picked up as a truant, and sent to Youth House, where the sense of nurturing was on the chilly side as well. He lived in a foster home for a time. There, Sullivan was guilty of "acting out," seeking attention in potentially harmful ways. He was a thief. Like many kids who had nothing, he stole so he could have his own things like everyone else.

But he was caught stealing and sent to live in B-2 Cottage at Warwick Reformatory in rural Warwick, N.Y., the middle of nowhere for a city kid. He was placed on the lawn-mowing squad. All of the other kids were sick in the head, some a lot worse than him. And they were all black, as were the adults who worked there, making Sullivan a natural target. Kids would beat him up because they were bored. He quickly learned to fight, and after a time was dishing out more than he took.

When he was fifteen he made repeated escape attempts, running through woods and swamps, but was always caught. Once he managed to steal a car and got back to New York City. After that they sent him to a series of institutions, each more soul sucking than the last—like descending further and further into hell: Elmira Reformatory, Coxsackie Reformatory, Napanoch, which was known in the vernacular of the day as an institution for "retard criminals." The only step further down was Mattawan State Mental Hospital where kids died weekly. At Napanoch, a bully tried to punk him but instead Sullivan busted his head with a piece of pipe. Nobody knew who did it. The kid was still in the hospital when Sullivan was released back into the public five months later, now a legal adult, and completely desensitized to violence. He wasn't a big guy—five-nine maybe, 170 pounds, with brown hair and hazel eyes—yet he had developed a persona that seemed straight out of old gangster movies, strutting like a tough guy and speaking with a gravelly voice.

Sullivan struggled with freedom. He was fired from three

jobs in eight days. The longest lasted four days and ended when he punched his supervisor in the face. He teamed up with a childhood friend turned heroin addict named Blackie and the pair hitchhiked out west while Blackie kicked the habit. (Before the days of rehab, junkies used to get clean in places where they knew there was no heroin, like the desert.) They made it to California, and then Las Vegas, Nevada, before being picked up in a cattle-freezing blizzard in Wyoming because Blackie resembled a Canadian bank robber. Sullivan was packing a Smith and Wesson .38 and was booked on gun charges. He and Blackie were separated by the cops and never teamed up again.

In jail Sullivan was told he was facing five years and so tried to escape out a window and fell to the ice below, breaking his shoulder and scraping so much skin off his face it took two years to heal. The attempt was so foolhardy that Cheyenne police mistook it for a suicide attempt. He was eventually sentenced to only twenty-two days on the gun charge and came to like the jail, which was much warmer than the icy Wyoming winter.

Once out and desperately in the need of shelter, he enlisted in the army in Colorado. He failed to make it through basic training, went AWOL, made it back to New York on a bus, but was only free in the city for forty-eight hours when he was caught and jailed in the circular bastion stockade of Governor's Island in New York Harbor.

It was a place thick with irony, a place where a jailbird could look out through the steel bars and see the Statue of Liberty.

For months he plotted escape, and trained by taking ice cold showers. He escaped in December by swimming across the near-frozen Buttermilk Channel to Brooklyn, used a knife to commandeer a ride from a cabbie to East New York where he hopped the turnstiles and caught an A train "home."

When he got home, only one brother was up but he gave Joseph dry clothes to change into.

He was caught again, spent six days in a tin box with a slot in it for food before getting out by setting his mattress on fire. They dragged him out and rendered him unconscious with a needle. He woke up to an interview with a psychologist during which he giggled inappropriately, earning him a stint in the mental wing of the Valley Forge Army Hospital. When his sanity returned, he was given a Bad Conduct Discharge and mustered out.

He tried without luck to find legit employment. He began a series of armed robberies but was caught. Less than a year after his release from Warwick, he was in the Hudson County Jail, convicted and sentenced to five-to-seven in Rahway Prison, where he was present for the riots.

As had become the pattern, Sullivan emerged from stir a more hardened criminal than when he went in, he began to deserve most-wanted status. On December 19, 1965, he shot and killed John Campbell, a father of eight, during a bar fight in Queens, N.Y., and went on the lam, committing brazen armed robberies in Texas, Georgia, Louisiana, and Alabama, before he was captured and returned to New York to face manslaughter charges while residing in the Queens County Jail.

In 1967, he was convicted of manslaughter, sentenced to twenty-to-thirty years, and sent to Attica, where he developed lung cancer and had to have a lung removed. After his operation, he worked very hard to get himself back into peak physical condition. According to a parole officer, Sullivan did a thousand pushups and ran ten miles a day. He didn't age like other prisoners, and eventually looked a full decade younger than he actually was.

Sullivan became the star running back for the Attica football team, which played in uniforms and used equipment donated by the Buffalo Bills. The pulling guard that blocked for Sullivan was a huge mob bodyguard named Thomas "Tommy the Eagle" Taylor, so nicknamed because of the intense look in his eyes. Although Sullivan would go thirteen years without seeing Taylor after he got out, his football buddy would turn out to be a very important part of his life.

On Good Friday, 1971, Sullivan buried himself in a pile of empty flour bags in the back of a truck that was leaving the prison, thus becoming the only prisoner to ever get over, under, or through that fortress's thirty-foot walls.

Interestingly, the flour-bags-in-the-truck story comes from another inmate, while Sullivan always maintained that he threw a rope and "climbed the wall."

Once out, everyone agrees that he approached a stranger in the prison parking lot, never identified, and hitched a ride to the bus station in Batavia. Sullivan's version, the less likely of the two, may have been concocted to protect accomplices.

Sullivan remained on the lam for five and a half weeks, was spotted once in the city of Rochester, N.Y., and was eventually apprehended on a hip Greenwich Village street, carrying a concealed sawed-off .22 rifle.

Weeks after his recapture, the New York State Supreme Court upheld Sullivan's manslaughter conviction, after an appeal stating that he had not been read his rights when he confessed to the shooting.

Despite the escape, Sullivan—with the help of former U.S. Attorney General Ramsay Clark as his lawyer—convinced a parole board to release him on parole in 1975, and his criminal career resumed.

He had done much thinking in prison and decided that, when he got out, he was going to become the world's greatest professional killer. He wouldn't just get the job done. He'd do it so it was untraceable to his employer. A skill like that, he figured, would put him in huge demand.

The Genovese crime family hired him first in 1976 to kill two members of the Irish crew run by mobster Mickey Spillane (not to be confused with the author of the Mike Hammer novels)—and his career as a hit man was off to a successful start.

One of those hits was the January 22, 1977 murder of Tom

"The Greek" Kapatos, a Spillane enforcer, on West 34th Street in Manhattan. Kapatos was a guy who spent most of his life in prison, first for murder, and then for a $3 million jewel heist.

In 1977 Sullivan married a Jewish girl named Gail Weiner, and they had two boys, Ramsay, named after the esteemed attorney who'd fought for Sullivan's freedom, and Kelly.

The man they called "Mad Dog", a nickname earned in prison reportedly because of an overactive salivary gland, was simultaneously a warm family man and a stone-cold killer.

On May 13, 1977, Spillane himself was whacked, shot from a dark sedan as he exited his home in Woodside, Queens. Again Sullivan was high on the suspect list, although he was never charged.

Sullivan was also reportedly assigned to kill Mafia boss Carmine Galante but his efforts failed, and when Galante was murdered in Brooklyn in 1978, it was by someone else.

As Sullivan's reputation grew, Sullivan and wife Gail thought of a legitimate way to profit from Joseph's supreme criminality—they would write a book. It was called *Tears and Tiers,* and glamorized life as a crook while omitting all mention of Joseph being a professional killer.

The book attracted the attention of movie producer Robert Schaffel, who called it "terrifying, devastating." There was talk for a time of making a movie with actor Jon Voight playing the Mad Dog. But that fell through when they learned that, in addition to stealing things, Sullivan was a suspect in seven murders.

One of those murders took place in June 1981 in New York City when Sullivan was with his wife. She had been arrested also but was released without bail to take care of her kids, while Joseph remained on the lam.

At one point that summer, Sullivan, Gail and the boys all stayed together at the cottage of football-buddy Thomas "Eagle" Taylor on Lake Ontario near the city of Rochester. While there, Sullivan met a couple of other local hoods, a Thomas Torpey, who had ambitions of being a big-time hood, and a man-mountain named Louis "Hulk" DiGiulio, so nicknamed because he had muscles on top of his muscles and resembled Lou Ferrigno.

Both Torpey and DiGiulio would prove to be part of Sullivan's final undoing.

As was common during the 1980s, Sullivan developed an expensive and debilitating cocaine habit. After a time he needed cocaine to stay alert and plenty of alcohol to stay calm, and eventually to fall asleep. The habit was wearying—and very expensive. He didn't have an answer for the first problem, but the second was easy. He went to where the money was.

At 9:05 Monday morning, December 14, 1981, Sullivan with a shotgun and another man with a pistol, entered the Marine Midland bank in Utica, N.Y., ordered the other customers to leave, and left with $14,000, escaping in a white Oldsmobile.

On December 8, 1981, Sullivan and thirty-four-year-old Marco Tedesco murdered thirty-seven-year-old Richard Bretz and his girlfriend, twenty-five-year-old Virginia Carson in Carson's Selden, N.Y. apartment, in Long Island's Suffolk County. A second man, thirty-eight-year-old Andrew Saldo, was severely wounded in that attack.

All three victims had had their throats cut after they were shot. The killings, police believed, were about drugs. That same day a drug store in Selden was held up for $300 in cash and $3,000 worth of opioid painkillers, presumably also by Sullivan and Tedesco. The pair was indicted for the double homicide after the grand jury visited the ICU of a Long Island hospital where Saldo testified he knew the killers because they had all hung out together at the same strip joint.

Which brings us back to where we started, Mad Dog calling his girlfriend to tell her he had a gig and he needed her help.

"We're going to Rochester. You're driving," he said.

Hours later they were on the road. Between Utica and Syracuse it began to snow. By the time they got to the West Henrietta Road exit, the roads were treacherous. Sullivan stashed the moll in a motel and split.

"I got to meet a guy," he said.

The target was John "Johnny Flowers" Fiorino, a good fellow with big-time union power. The motive was complicated, a combo of these factors: 1) Fiorino was a rat; 2) Fiorino sponsoring a merger that would have left Taylor and Torpey on the outside; and 3) Fiorino demanded excessive tribute—referred to by the wise guys as "juice."

The guy Sullivan had to meet was twenty-five-year-old Louis A. "Hulk" DiGiulio. He wasn't that bright but knew Rochester streets and could I.D. Fiorino. Sullivan gave DiGiulio the car keys. DiGiulio told Sullivan not to worry about the snow. People in Rochester were used to it. He drove Sullivan to a Marriott hotel in Greece for a meeting with Torpey and Taylor, where the men deep nostrilled two grams of coke and made the contract.

Thomas Torpey

Taylor said, "Could you do me another favor?"

"Depends," Sullivan said.

"I got a place called Show World Peep Show on State Street, own it under another name. I can't be seen there. Could you drop off some quarters for me?"

Sullivan was offended at first that Taylor would ask a man of his stature to perform such a menial task, but then decided it was funny and agreed.

Before getting into Sullivan's Caddy, Mad Dog opened the trunk and pulled out a license plate with magnets fixed to its back. He put the magnetic plates over his own.

"Just in case," he said.

"Smart," DiGiulio said with a nervous smile.

Sullivan was thinking this guy wouldn't know smart if it bit him on the nose.

After the peep show, where he could feel the clap crawling up his leg, it was off to a series of bars, looking for the target. At one place DiGiulio saw a guy he wanted to beat up but Sullivan talked him out of it, saying he had to look at the big picture.

Moments later, while driving an open stretch of road, Sullivan stuck the sawed-off Marlin twelve-gauge pump-action shotgun out the window and fired. DiGiulio jumped out of his skin.

"Easy. Just making sure it works," Sullivan said with a laugh.

They pulled over at a phone booth. DiGiulio dropped a quarter and made a call.

"One more stop, Big Guy. I think this is it," DiGiulio said.

The stop was The Blue Gardenia. Word was Johnny Flowers was expected. Dark, dreamy music drifted out of the joint, a sax and piano wandering from the tonic to the dominant chord in the company of a minor7.

The parking lot was packed. Torpey and Taylor were inside at a table, close to a window and facing the door.

"Not here yet," DiGiulio said, scanning the luxury cars in the lot.

"What now?" Sullivan asked.

"We wait."

They didn't have to wait long. Sullivan had the shotgun across his lap, when Fiorino pulled into the lot in his Lincoln.

"That's the guy," DiGiulio said.

Sullivan got out of the car, approached his target from behind. He walked quickly at first, shoulders braced against the wind, then broke into a jog. He raised the shotgun, fired, and struck his target high on the shoulder, knocking Fiorino down.

The victim was on the ground clawing clumsily at an ankle holster where he kept a .38 snub. Sullivan approached with soft steps, pointed the barrel down at Johnny Flower's contorted face. He leaned over and fired point blank. Blue flame came from the shotgun, and a full load of double-O buck destroyed Fiorino's head.

Sullivan briskly returned to the Caddy, which was already moving. As soon as Sullivan got both feet in the car, DiGiulio spun the tires and peeled out.

"Easy. No hurry," Sullivan said. "Turn your lights on!"

But DiGiulio couldn't be easy. The car squealed and fishtailed its way onto Empire Boulevard with its lights off—directly in front of the patrol car of Irondequoit cop Michael

DiGiovanni, who saw what he believed to be a drunk driver leaving a bar. DiGiovanni hit the lights and siren.

Sullivan cursed and reloaded his shotgun.

The road was icy, visibility poor. With a police car now in pursuit, DiGiulio drove erratically. He ran a red light, was clipped by another car in the right rear, skidded, hit a curb, and bounced to a stop on the grassy strip between the street and the sidewalk near Helendale Road. The cop car efficiently sealed off the path to get back on the street and the men were trapped.

"Here," Sullivan said, handing DiGiulio his .38 Cobra. "We got to shoot it out."

DiGiulio popped out of the car, and fell hard on a patch of ice. Sullivan could tell his driver wasn't going to help him fight. All he saw was DiGiulio's broad back as made a run for it, comically falling several times before he disappeared behind a house. Sullivan emerged more carefully, holding the shotgun with both hands.

Officer DiGiovanni saw the shotgun and got his head down fast. He stretched out on his front seat and kicked open his driver-side door. In response, Sullivan emptied both barrels on the cop car, blowing a gaping hole in the door and shattering the windshield. DiGiovanni felt pieces of glass raining down onto his head.

After a moment of quiet, the cop emerged revolver in hand, and returned fire, six shots, emptying his gun. He saw Sullivan lurch and thought he'd hit him. (He had, but Sullivan's bulletproof vest saved his life.) The cop retreated to reload and call for back up. When he popped back out, Sullivan was gone, disappeared.

Sullivan found DiGiulio behind the house.

"You hit?"

"No, just can't run in the snow."

"Is this the way?" Sullivan asked.

"I dunno," DiGiulio said with a shrug.

Sullivan cursed and hopped a fence. DiGiulio followed,

but when he got on the other side, Sullivan was nowhere to be seen.

On Empire Boulevard, back-up arrived. Officer Theresa Young guarded the cars while DiGiovanni and Officer Mark Bonsignore chased the assailants, following the two sets of footprints in the snow through the backyard of a house on Queensboro Road.

The policemen could see the fence had been hopped. There was still snow on the fence and wood was broken in one spot. A hat, which turned out to be Sullivan's, was found at that spot.

Irondequoit cop Michael DiGiovanni

They quickly found DiGiulio hiding in the bushes in a gully behind a nearby school, only feet from Interstate 590. He was arraigned in a locked and secured courtroom.

Sullivan, on the other hand, had vanished. He later claimed he buried himself in a snowdrift and stayed there for up to two hours, listening as searching police and K-9 teams came within feet of him.

When he was certain they were gone he dug himself out, brushed himself off, and went into a nearby bar full of mob wannabes watching news of the hit on TV. Sullivan called a friend who came and got him and drove him fifty miles to the Buffalo airport.

Police staked out mobby locations, including Torpey's Young Men's Social Club, a gambling parlor on Lyell Avenue. They hauled in a half-dozen known gangsters and grilled them. The Rochester and Irondequoit police worked the case in conjunction with the U.S. Organized Crime Strike Force.

In the trunk of Sullivan's Caddy police found more that $6,000 in cash, a .32 caliber automatic with a silencer, bullets, a navy pinstripe suit with scarlet handkerchief in the breast pocket, and a Valentine's Day card. In the back seat was a leather traveling case with brass fittings, and targets for pistol practice. Opening up the travel case, police expected to find a comb, razor and maybe nail clippers. Instead it held live shotgun shells, prescription painkillers, and an I.D. with Sullivan's photo under a fake name.

Two months passed. For cops, the break came on February 23, 1982: Sullivan was back in Rochester, looking to be paid for the Fiorino hit, staying at the Denonville Inn, room 3, in Webster.

He was with his girlfriend, Theresa. They had again driven to Rochester together, this time in her car. He'd quit shaving and was wearing a full beard.

Someone in the Denonville bar had a good memory for faces and called 911.

While it was still dark, cops staked out the place, a cozy strip of motel rooms attached at one end to an A-frame house. The sun came up, although it didn't get very bright. The snow worsened, now blowing across the motel parking lot in squalls.

Sullivan left his room to go to Theresa's car at about 10:20 a.m. carrying two green suitcases. He put them in the trunk of the blue Ford and went back into the room. He stepped out a second time, this time empty handed, returned to the car, and ten armed FBI agents surrounded him.

The G-Men worked the motel room for a few hours, and split. Housekeeping put it back together to ready it for the next guest, a bit of a chore as the mattresses were turned over and the toilet dismantled.

News of the capture spread quickly and by the time Sullivan got to the federal building on State Street, there was a pack of press boys waiting. He was offered an opportunity to hide his face but replied he had nothing to be ashamed of—and so he made the perp walk from the car to the building with head high. He coursed a gauntlet of flashing strobes, whirring cameras and shouting reporters.

"Why did you kill Fiorino? Was it a mob hit?"

"I didn't kill nobody," Mad Dog said.

Sullivan was booked and placed in the Monroe County jail. They caged him as far as they could get him from DiGiulio, who had resided there since the night at The Blue Gardenia.

Sullivan pleaded not guilty to murder and attempted murder in Monroe County Court. But his days of freedom were done. He died in prison in 2017.

On March 2, Theresa's sister Marie posted $2,500 cash to bail her out, and the pair returned to Brooklyn.

On April 6, a Torpey confederate named Howard Ferren was found slumped in his car with bullets in his arm and his wooden leg, causing disagreement over whether he'd been shot once or twice.

For the Rochester mob war, the whacking of Fiorino and the capture of Sullivan spelled the beginning the end. The C team turned out to be short-lived, guys getting hit in 1982 and 1983, all of the shootings in the Rochester suburb of Gates. A guy named Tony Olivari turned informant, and his info wiped out the A team in 1984. Torpey and Taylor went to prison in 1985.

After the trial, Gail Sullivan re-issued her husband's biography, updated to include events since the first printing. In it Sullivan admitted he killed Fiorino—but told a story that protected the two Thomases. They had nothing to do with it. In Sullivan's parallel universe, he did it to help DiGiulio, who he said was a gambler deeply in debt to Fiorino. DiGiulio was afraid that he would be whacked, and Sullivan removed the threat. DiGiulio returned the favor by testifying against him in court. The driver couldn't drive, Sullivan said. His greatest skill was "pretending."

Nobody bought it. Sullivan killed for a living. The thought that he'd take the risk to save a degenerate gambler's skin was laughable.

Stephanie Joy Kupchynsky

PURE/EVIL

Stephanie Joy Kupchynsky was already famous, in a positive way, years before her name became another tragic synonym for sadness. She was one of the violin-playing Kupchynsky sisters, virtuosos, under the tutelage of their music-teacher dad, Jerry.

Jerry Kupchynsky, who emigrated from the Ukraine in the 1950s, was the music supervisor of the East Brunswick, New Jersey, school system. He and his wife had two daughters, and Jerry ended up raising them alone because his wife was stricken with multiple sclerosis, and had to be institutionalized in 1976. Mom remained in the institution for two decades before she passed away.

In 1978, Stephanie and her sister Melanie were the concertmistress and first concertmistress of the Central New

Jersey High School Orchestra. That orchestra, an all-star team chosen after more than one-thousand auditions, played on January 8, 1978, before a packed house at the Metuchen High School auditorium. The concert began with "The Star-Spangled Banner" followed by the winter concerto from Vivaldi's "The Four Seasons." Stephanie and Melanie were the only siblings in the orchestra.

After completing high school in the East Brunswick public school system, Stephanie attended West Virginia University and Boston's New England Conservatory of Music.

By 1982, the sisters were still playing together, the featured musicians in an orchestra that played a free concert presented by the Society of Musical Arts at the Millburn Library. Among the pieces they played that day were the Bach Double Concerto, during which Stephanie and Melanie took turns as soloists, and works by Handel and Boccherini.

In 1985, Stephanie was a featured performer without her sister in Putney, Vermont, playing a tribute to American composer George Crumb at the Yellow Barn Music Festival. The concert was held at the Putney Federated Church on Tuesday evening, July 30.

By 1988, Stephanie no longer needed an orchestra around her to perform. She was doing concerts by herself, mostly back in New Jersey where she grew up, including a series of shows sponsored by the East Brunswick Arts Commission.

Before moving to the Rochester area, she taught the violin for two years on Martha's Vineyard in Massachusetts.

Then, the sadness.

During the summer of 1991, older sister Melanie was in Chicago playing with the Chicago Symphony Orchestra, while twenty-seven-year-old Stephanie was living in the Rochester, N.Y. suburb of Greece, and working as a fourth and fifth grade music teacher at three Greece schools—West Ridge, Buckman Heights, and Lakeshore—where her students called her Miss K.

She looked younger than she was and her fellow teachers used to kid her that they couldn't tell the kids from the teacher when she was in front of a class.

And it was in the Flower City that Stephanie disappeared. Her boyfriend Ken Sullivan of Ithaca said he last spoke to her on Wednesday, July 31. Also on that Wednesday she left a message on her father's phone answering machine. She was last seen that same evening when she stopped at a neighborhood grocery store to pick up a few items on her way home from a girlfriend's apartment. She was supposed to teach a private violin lesson on August 1, but when her student arrived at her apartment in the Newcastle Apartments on Kingsberry Drive she wasn't there. The student left a note on the door.

Stephanie's red 1985 Nissan Sentra was found parked in the long-term parking lot at the Greater Rochester International Airport on Friday, August 2. In the car was her wallet, with credit cards in it but no cash.

The investigation into Stephanie's disappearance had barely begun when it turned gloomy. On August 3, a nineteen-year-old Kendall, N.Y., man found Stephanie's checkbook on the shoulder of Route 260 in Hamlin not far from Lake Ontario, a location that was not between Stephanie's apartment and the airport. The guy's name was Christopher Mosher and he, bizarrely, forged three checks from the book and cashed two, before turning the remaining checks in to the police. He said he didn't know Stephanie.

Cops grilled Mosher for many hours before coming to the conclusion that he was telling the truth and knew nothing about Stephanie's disappearance. Bloodhounds searched the area where the checkbook was found with no positive results.

Stephanie's family dismissed any notion that Stephanie would have traveled without telling anyone (and leave her credit cards behind). She had been scheduled to attend a music conference at Glassboro State College in New Jersey. She didn't show up. Stephanie was gone. Worse, someone had taken Stephanie.

On August 6, the Greece police said they had leads regarding Stephanie's disappearance but offered no details. Those leads, however, did not pan out. By August 8, Greece police were freely admitting that they didn't know why Stephanie was missing. They were quick to point out that there was no evidence of foul play.

Well, no physical evidence. There was no blood. No sign of a struggle anywhere. There was certainly *circumstantial* evidence of foul play. There was the checkbook in Hamlin. She had left her pet birds unattended. Her credit cards were in her car, and no cash withdrawals had been made from her bank account. If she was ok, how was she paying for things?

Nope, something bad had happened.

As sister Melanie put it, "Stephanie had no pressing problems. She had no reason to flee. She had just had her car serviced for the drive to New Jersey. Everything was going so well for her. There's nothing that's ever happened to her that she's not told me about. All these facts add up to a really bad picture. She has never done anything like this before. It's absolutely unthinkable that she would have left without telling anyone. She wouldn't have done this to mother."

By the middle of August, police were publicizing a description of Stephanie. Along with her photo, the public now knew she was five-four, one-twenty, with light brown hair and brown eyes.

By the end of August, Greece school officials were meeting to decide how to go about telling Stephanie's students that she was gone, maybe gone forever, and no one knew what had happened to her.

No one had any good ideas. Maybe just tell the truth. Stephanie's co-worker and friend Kathleen Sullivan said, "I don't look forward to discussing it at length with children. I don't want to think about it. Everyone is just sick about it. It's something very strange. I don't think we will ever know why she disappeared."

The school district quietly placed Stephanie on a leave of absence and hired a new violin teacher. Letters went out to the parents of Stephanie's young students offering tips on coping with the sad mystery. School psychologists from other districts were called in to help.

The Greece PTA sent food to Stephanie's apartment, where her family was staying during the search. There was talk of chipping in and hiring a private detective to help the police with the search. Then it was learned that the family had already hired a private eye, Michael Giardina who charged $40 per hour, so the PTA decided to help the family with the cost. A fund was set up and pleas for contributions appeared in the daily papers. Melanie told reporters the family was "desperate and helpless."

Dad Jerry said, "We've played hundreds of different scenarios of what may have happened. I think she was abducted. But she is pretty tough. As long as the worst hasn't happened, I feel she will turn up somewhere, somehow."

Jerry explained that the other possibility was that Stephanie had taken her own life, and she'd done it in a way in which finding her was difficult or impossible. She had been treated for depression for "several years."

She had started taking Prozac while teaching on Martha's Vineyard. She blamed the winter, telling her dad that the Vineyard was paradise in the summer but a "hell hole" in the winter. She had taken the anti-depressant drug for years but had stopped shortly before she disappeared. Maybe that was the key clue.

Jerry explained, "I spoke to her only a few days before she disappeared, and at that particular point in her life she had never been in better shape emotionally—or at least she seemed so."

Back in Rochester, you couldn't go very far without seeing a poster with Stephanie's photo on it. Psychics were brought in but the information they provided led nowhere.

The Greece Police Department had to deal with a handful of

false leads. An anonymous caller reported seeing Stephanie in a Dunkin Donuts, but hung up before giving other details and did not call back despite pleas to do so in the *Democrat & Chronicle*.

By December, Greece police had moved on to other things. They told Stephanie's family that she had simply "left her life." Jerry Kupchynsky hadn't given up, though. He offered a $5,000 reward for anyone providing information that led to finding Stephanie. In 1992, that reward rose to $10,000.

During the autumn of 1992 an almost "full skeleton" was discovered in the town of Hamlin, not far from where Stephanie's checkbook had been found. The discovery was made by a group of boys, two thirteen-year-olds and nine-year-old Curtis Musson, who were looking for soft drink cans off the Lake Ontario State Parkway.

"I looked in the bushes and it was just sitting there," Musson said. "I couldn't believe it. We stood there for like fifty seconds. For a while we thought maybe it was a deer, but then we decided it was a person and we better tell someone about it."

They told other kids, who came to look at the bones and offer their opinion. It was a while before one of the boys mentioned the find to an adult and the adult called the police. Musson's mom shivered when she heard about it. She remembered walking by that same spot during the summer and smelling a bad odor. Now she knew what it was.

That area had been a hotbed for criminal activity. The body of thirty-four-year-old Glenda Crittenden, last seen getting into a red pickup truck, was found two miles from there in Parma on September 3, 1992, and the body of thirty-two-year-old Patricia Grimes was found in a ditch off Chase Road near there in 1990.

Dental records were used to determine that the newly discovered skeleton was not Stephanie. It had only been a year since Rochester-area serial killer Arthur Shawcross had been sentenced to 250-years in prison for the eleven murders he'd admitted to, and now there were fears that a new serial killer was at work.

"Yes, I think we have a problem," said Captain Neil Flood, the commander of the Monroe County Major Crimes Unit. "We've got three dead girls within two miles of each other. That's a strong indication that something's going on."

There were similarities in the remains that had nothing to do with geography. Two had been strangled and the third was presumed to have been strangled. All were found nude and dumped in a remote location, yet beyond the remoteness of the dumpsite no attempt had been made to hide the remains.

The problem up near Hamlin got worse. Another body, that of Cindy Marie Thiele, twenty-nine years old, was found near West Wautoma Road on October 10. Two weeks later, thirty-six-year-old Betty Jean Gaddy was found north of the parkway in Hamlin, near East Wautoma Beach Road. Gaddy had a criminal record as a sex worker.

Three other young women were missing, all disappeared in 1992: Janine Clausen who disappeared in February, Sandra Johnson missing since August, and Victoria Jobson who disappeared in October. (The Victoria Jobson case is discussed in detail in my book, with Donald A. Tubman, *Haunting Homicides*.)

But none of this seemed to have anything to do with Stephanie Kupchynsky, who by all accounts had zero experience "on the street." (Some of these cases were later linked with presumed serial killer John White, an electrician who lived on Trolley Boulevard in Gates, and was known to pick up sex workers on Lyell Avenue in his red pickup truck, the same location where Shawcross had picked up the majority of his victims. Women who had gotten into White's truck and lived to tell about it said that he never wanted sex, but always quizzed them as to their age, place of residence, and number of friends and family in the area. He did this with hostility in his eyes. One woman said that a black man in a red pickup truck had picked her up and attacked her, tried to strangle her, but she managed to get away. She and the other women who'd been in the red truck positively identified White as the man, and all agreed that he kept a Bible on his dashboard. When he was put under twenty-four-hour surveillance for four months, the killings stopped. While still under surveillance, White died of a heart attack and never admitted to being a killer.)

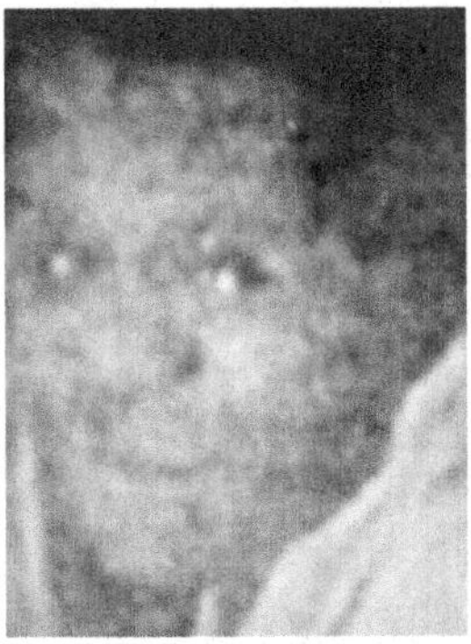

John White

In 1996, Stephanie's mom, Jean, long ill and institutionalized, passed away, never knowing her daughter's fate.

The hunt for Stephanie ended on April 15, 1998, almost seven years after she disappeared, when two boys chasing a fish down a stream in Orleans County—just west of the Monroe County line, about a thousand yards off of Hurd Road in the town of Murray, and a half-mile south of Route 104—discovered her skeletal remains. There had been no attempt to hide the bones. No clothes or personal items were found nearby.

The boys who found Stephanie's bones were thirteen-year-old Justin Whipple and eleven-year-old Chris Weber, both of Holley, N.Y. They wouldn't have found the stream at all if the dirt bike they'd been riding had not stalled nearby the day before. They found the stream at that time and decided to return the next day because it looked like a good place to fish.

The creek was a branch of Sandy Creek, and was only two and a half feet wide at the spot where the remains were found.

Weber described the scene: "It was about five o'clock. I was hopping from log to log, then I sat down and I saw it. We knew it was a skull. We couldn't think of any other animal it could have been besides a human."

Other bones in the water accompanied the skull, and after a little searching they found additional bones on the ground beside the creek. The boys poked at the remains with a stick for a moment and then felt frightened and fled.

Weber said it was the most scared he'd ever been. The boys ran home but didn't immediately tell anyone what they had found. They were afraid that they would get in trouble. They weren't sure who owned the land they were on and worried that they'd be arrested and charged with trespassing.

"It was about nine o'clock that night, I told my big brother and he said I should tell our parents," Whipple said. "I told my dad but he thought I was kidding, that it was some kind of a prank. I told him I'd prove it, so my dad grabbed a flashlight and we went back there. My dad saw the bones and said, 'Good God! I didn't believe you!'"

The Orleans County Sheriff's Department was then notified and Whipple and his dad again returned to the scene, this time accompanied by investigators. As there was no one in Orleans County missing, someone suggested they call the Greece police, as they still had some of the Stephanie Kupchynsky missing posters lying around.

Once the remains were identified as Stephanie's, Greece police called Melanie in Chicago and she called her father. Jerry told a reporter, "There were times when I would tell myself I wanted to know what happened and just put the whole case to sleep, but there were other times I thought I didn't want to know, that it was better if I could hold onto a little hope. I've been bleeding emotionally for the whole time, so in a way, I'm relieved because there's closure now. Even though the little spark of hope I maintained all this time that she was alive was extinguished, I'm relieved."

The Greece police told the press that they had a "primary suspect," although they did not identify him. He was, they said, someone who was familiar with the Newcastle Apartments on Kingsberry Drive where Stephanie lived.

The suspect, they said, had been released from prison in January 1991 after serving time for robbery. That ex-con also had a prior sex offense on his record.

He had been a primary suspect during the first weeks after Stephanie disappeared. Police secretly tailed the suspect and paced a tracking device on his car in case he shook his tail. The surveillance bore almost immediate fruit as police saw him in the process of attacking a teenaged girl on Monroe Avenue, and intervened to save the intended victim.

The suspect yelled for a lawyer before police could question him. Regarding the unfinished attack, the suspect was convicted of first-degree sexual abuse and was sentenced to twenty-five-year-to-life sentence as a persistent violent felon. If police wanted to question him again, they would know where he was. His name was "common knowledge" among police, it was said. The Kupchynskys knew the name of the suspect through their private investigator, Mike Giardina.

Edward G. Laraby

The suspect was Edward G. Laraby, forty-five years old, and a maintenance worker at the Newcastle Apartments at the time of Stephanie's disappearance. He had been released from prison six months before Stephanie disappeared. Although Laraby had never admitted to being responsible for Stephanie's disappearance, he did once try to make a deal, through his attorney Michael Schiano, in which he said he would trade info regarding Stephanie for a lighter sentence. Now that Stephanie's remains had been found, Schiano tried to play down his client's offering of a deal.

"There was never any discussion of leading anyone to a body or anything like that," Schiano said. It was hard to imagine what information Laraby wanted to trade if he was going to deny being her killer.

Monroe County District Attorney Howard Relin refused to verify that Laraby was the suspect in question, but he did say, "Our hope is that he never gets out of jail. He is one of the most dangerous individuals we've ever had."

A look at Laraby's record confirmed Relin's opinion. At about 11:00 p.m. on October 19, 1973, twenty-year-old Laraby, while wearing a ski mask, picked up a fifteen-year-old Pittsford girl as she hitchhiked on Marsh Road in Perinton. He took her to a railroad station near Lyndon Road in Perinton, tied her hands, gagged her mouth, cut her clothes off with a knife, and then raped her. When she resisted, he beat her with a belt and pressed the knife to her neck. He left her bound and gagged, her clothes in a pile beside her. She wore eyeglasses, so Laraby put her glasses on her outside the blindfold. She worked her way free and ran a mile before flagging down a passing motorist. The crime was called by police "blatantly vicious."

On November 12, 1973, he repeated the crime, this time with a seventeen-year-old girl whom he picked up at the Twelve Corners in Brighton and raped at the Cobbs Hill Reservoir.

He was arrested, tried, convicted, and sentenced to six-and-a-half to twenty-five years in prison. In 1974 he was sent to Attica to serve his term, but was released in 1980 when he appealed his conviction on the grounds that his lawyer was incompetent for failing to challenge the legality of a police lineup, and for failing to interview Laraby's alibi witnesses.

He was only back on the streets for a matter of weeks when he forced a seventeen-year-old girl into his car at knifepoint and forced her to commit sodomy at the corner of Alexander Street and Monroe Avenue.

He was again arrested, released on bail, and fled. He made it as far as Rolla, North Dakota, population 1,458, where no one had seen a stranger in years. Authorities kept an eye on the stranger in town and he was re-arrested when he tried to cross the border into Canada.

Laraby was plenty evil but not that bright, said Monroe County Assistant District Attorney Charles Siragusa. "If he really wanted to go to Canada, he could have walked across the Peace Bridge in Niagara Falls and no one would have noticed him," Siragusa said.

In February of 1981 he pleaded guilty to first-degree sexual abuse and was sentenced to two-to-seven years in prison. He went to prison but was released after only one month because he was given credit for the time he served at Attica before his conviction was overturned.

In October of 1983 he put on a scary Halloween mask, and spent the day hiding behind hedges and jumping out to frighten women with a knife in his hand as they walked the bicycle path along the Erie (then called the Barge) Canal in Brighton. Eventually he bored of this and robbed a Henrietta woman who was walking the path. The woman was with her daughter at the time. He took her car keys, credit cards, and pocketbook.

The break in the Stephanie Kupchynsky case came when a fellow named Burton Verhay, a former lieutenant detective with the MCSO, was having dinner with Chief of Detectives Gerald Barker. They got to talking about the canal attacks and Verhay said, "Sounds like Laraby. Is he out?"

The answer was yes, but not for long. In February 1984 he was arrested for the canal crimes, and was sentenced to four-to-eight years in prison. Judge Donald Wisner said he wished he could put Laraby away for good.

"You have a real sickness," the judge said.

He served six years and in 1991 was back on the street and working at the Newcastle Apartments when Stephanie disappeared.

On August 14, 1992, he raped a sixteen-year-old girl who he'd abducted as she walked along Monroe Avenue. He was again caught and tried. A prosecutor said, "Instead of hunting animals, the defendant hunts women. He is a predator. It's my opinion, were it not for the intervention of the officers who had been stalking you, that you would have killed that young lady."

This time Laraby was sent away for good, as a repeat violent felon. He would serve his time at the Auburn Correctional Facility.

The Orleans County Sheriff's Department immediately removed Stephanie's bones from the narrow stream and, using a backhoe, three yards of soil from the crime scene and took it back to the sheriff's office.

They failed, however, to either rope off or leave a guard on the scene overnight, so that any future evidence that might be found near the dump site could be deemed tainted should a suspect be arrested and go to trial. Some defense attorneys said that it would be difficult to convict anyone after making that kind of a mistake with the evidence, but others said the error was mitigated by the fact that so much time had elapsed between the dumping of the body and its discovery.

Although the place where the bones were found was immediately assumed to be a crime scene, there was no physical evidence of foul play. There was just an assumption based on the fact that the bones were found in a place where Stephanie would not have gone on her own, that all of her clothes were missing, and her car was many miles away in the airport parking lot.

In July 1998, it was announced that Orleans County Coroner Scott Schmidt's autopsy of Stephanie's remains was inconclusive. He said the case was now officially a homicide because of the circumstances not because of his autopsy, which failed to reveal a cause of death.

The bones were sent to Dr. William Rodriguez, a forensic anthropologist with the Armed Forces Institute of Pathology outside Washington, D.C. His study of the bones was inconclusive as well. He sent the bones to the Monroe County morgue, where they were to be held until there was an arrest, at which time the remains would be turned over to the Kupchynsky family.

In the meantime, the lead investigator, Sgt. David Connors of the Greece police, was concentrating on linking his primary suspect, Laraby, with the victim. In October 1998, the Greece police sought the help of the FBI with the case. Sgt. Connors traveled to FBI headquarters for what he called an "investigative strategy session." He said that the feds "validated" what they had already been doing, which was focusing on Laraby.

During the first week of December 1998, Stephanie's remains were finally buried back home in New Jersey. Sister Melanie said, "It's amazing to me, after seven years how bad I still feel about it. It's something that never goes away. The tormenting thought to me was that she was out in the wild, in all kinds of weather. Now I feel a little bit comforted by this (burial), it's peaceful and it's final."

Stephanie's obituary ran in the December 10 issue of the *Central New Jersey Home News*. At 9:00 p.m. on December 9, there was a wake for Stephanie held at Maliszewski Memorial Home in South River, N.J. A funeral service was held on December 12 at St. Thomas Church in Old Bridge. She was buried next to her mother in Vincentown.

In July 2001, Laraby was out of his prison cell and in the coronary care unit at Auburn Memorial Hospital. On his sixth day in the hospital he attacked his guard. He took the wires that connected him to his heart monitors and managed to wrap them around the guard's neck. Laraby was subdued by hospital security before he could seriously injure the guard, and was taken immediately back to the Auburn Correctional Facility. He was later tried and convicted of attempted murder for attacking the hospital guard.

Twelve years later, on May 30, 2012, Laraby finally fessed up that he had killed Stephanie. By this time he had nothing to lose. He was dying of ALS, and confessed from his hospice bed at the Wende Correctional Facility. News of the confession leaked through Laraby's attorney Robert Napier. Laraby, he said, did not want the prison system to make his funeral arrangements, and in exchange for the right to make his own funeral plans Laraby admitted to killing Stephanie. Laraby was arraigned on the new charge of first-degree murder in the prison on July 16, 2012. At the arraignment Laraby pleaded not guilty. (Which made no sense, of course. He was thumbing his nose at the justice system even from his deathbed.)

During March 2013, Rochester area cab driver Joan Lenhard, and director of transportation for several of my books, picked up Robert Napier at the airport in her cab. She told him that she was a friend of Michael Benson, the true-crime writer, who was always poking around Rochester murders.

Napier reportedly said, "Have him get in touch with me. I have a story to tell him."

Apparently Napier changed his mind. I did make several attempts to contact him, all of which were sidestepped or ignored.

I researched Laraby for the first time after getting Joan's tip. By this time he was sixty years old and unable to walk. I found that he first made the papers in 1967, when he was only fourteen, because he was a hero—a story that had to be looked at in a new light now that we knew what a creep he became. In the spring of that year, a shed behind the Laraby house on Fellows Road in Perinton caught fire and Ed managed to save six of the twenty-five rabbits that lived there as pets. The rabbits were being raised, he said, "as sort of a family hobby." He'd been babysitting his younger brothers when the shed caught fire, cause unknown. Firefighters from Fairport and Egypt put the fire out.

Laraby's trial for Stephanie's murder never took place. It was postponed indefinitely because of his deteriorating health. On May 4, 2014, Laraby died of Lou Gehrig's disease, taking with him whatever secrets he had kept.

And yet his story was not through. According to defense lawyers working for James Krauseneck, who is under arrest for the 1982 ax murder of his wife in Brighton (another crime featured in *Haunting Homicides*), said that Laraby was the actual killer. The evidence, they claimed, was a confession to the crime that Laraby allegedly made in 2014, only days before he died.

In 2013, Melanie Kupchynsky and fellow musician and journalist Joanne Lipman published a book entitled *Strings Attached* (Hachette Books), about Melanie's dad Jerry, an immigrant who thought he'd found the American dream, who made a difference for hundreds of students as a music teacher, and then suffered a nightmare when Stephanie disappeared.

SOURCES

For *Killer Of The Cloth:*

Michael Benson. *The Devil at Genesee Junction."* Lanham, Maryland: Rowman & Littlefield, 2015.

Roy Elliot. "Woman Shot, Found Dead in River; Police Seek Identity Clue in Mystery." *D&C,* April 24, 1949, p.1.

"Cops Fail to Identify Body of Slain Woman." *D&C,* April 25, 1949, p. 2.

"Slain Woman from Oakland, Cal." *D&C,* April 26, 1949, p. 1.

Del Ray. "Cleric Held in River Death; Identifies Victim as Wife." *Rochester Times-Union,* April 26, 1949, p. 1.

Roy Elliot. "Buffalo Suburb Cleric Held in River Slaying Inquiry; Bullet in Automobile Matches Those in Wife's Body; Mystery Witness Quizzed, Views Prisoner at Jail." *D&C,* April 27, 1949, p. 1.

Roy Elliot. "Hetenyi Charged as Murder of Wife; Probers Place Slaying in Monroe County." *D&C,* April 28, 1949, p. 1.

Pat Fallon. "Asked Jean to Wait, Says Her Mother." *D&C,* April 28, 1949, p. 1.

Roy Elliot. "Gun Holster Found as Clue; Hetenyi Seen Along River, Mystery Witness Reveals." *D&C,* April 29, 1949, p. 1.

Roy Elliot. "Hetenyi Probing Centers on Loose Ends in Buffalo." *D&C,* April 30, 1949, p. 1.

Roy Elliot. "2nd Witness Places Hetenyi in Rochester On Night Before Wife's Body Was Found: Bloodstained Bit of Cloth Near River Site Adds to Evidence Chain." *D&C,* May 1, 1949, p. 1.

Bob Fischer. "New Witness Found, Last to Report Seeing Hetenyi with His Wife." *D&C,* May 2, 1949, p. 1.

______. "Police Guard Assigned To Hetenyi Burial Today; Deposit of Letter Bared." *D&C,* May 3, 1949, p. 1.

Bill Beeney. "Accused Cleric Remains Calm at Wife's Rite; Slaying Victim's Funeral Draws Throngs of Curious." *D&C,* May 4, 1949, p. 21.

Roy Elliot. "Hetenyi to Face Mental Tests At State Hospital Here Today." *D&C,* May 5, 1949, p. 25.

"Mental Quiz on Hetenyi." D&C, May 7, 1949, p. 15.

"Grand Jury to Get Hetenyi Case Today." *D&C,* May 10, 1949, p. 13.

"O'Mara Reserves Decision on Hetenyi Facts Request; Dr. Jaenike Finds Paranoid Tendencies During Interviews." *D&C,* November 1, 1949, p. 21.

Ruth Reynolds. "Second Degree Murder Conviction Is Changed to First in New Trial." *The Sunday Press* (Binghamton, N.Y.), June 24, 1951, p. 6D.

"Hetenyi To Get 4th Trial." *D&C,* February 22, 1966, p. B1.

"Lawyers Ask Hetenyi Charge Be Dismissed." D&C, May 4, 1966, p. B1.

Bill Claiborne. "'It's Over' - - Hetenyi's Now Free to Become Monk." *D&C,* June 2, 1966, p. B1.

"Hetenyi's Plea: 'It's Over…Please Leave Me Alone.'" *D&C,* June 7, 1966, p. 1C.

Michael R. Wolford. Trials & Tribulations: The Hetenyi murder trial: A Case For the Ages." *The Daily Record,* April 3, 2008, p. 1.

* * *

For *The Baby in the Convent:*

Marcia Bullard. "Can't recall doing anything to hurt the baby, nun testifies." *D&C,* March 2, 1977, p. A1.

______. "Doctor says nun's womb was normal." *D&C,* February 24, 1977, p. A1.

______. "Grand Jury will quiz head nun." *D&C,* May 25, 1976, p. B6.

______. "Knew I was pregnant, nun told grand jury." *D&C,* February 25, 1977, p. A1.

______. "Never heard baby cry, nun quoted." *D&C,* Febriary 18, 1977, p. A1.

______. "Nun arraigned in death." *D&C,* May 7, 1976, p. B1.

______. "Nun verdict is possible this morning." *D&C,* March 4, 1977, p. A1.

______. "Sister Maureen testifies." *D&C,* May 27, 1976, p. B6.

______. "Trial begins of nun in baby death." *D&C,* February 17, 1977, p. A1.

"Hearing delayed for nun charged in infant's death." *D&C,* May 18, 1976, p. B5.

Edward Hendrie. *Murder, Rape, and Torture in a Catholic Nunnery.* Great Mountain Publishing, 2015.

"Infant's body still in morgue." *D&C,* June 7, 1976, p. B2.

"Nun Acquitted in Death of Newborn Son ay N.Y. State Convent." *Washington Post,* March 5, 1977, p. 9.

"Nun Cleared of Charge She Killed Newborn Son." *New York Times*, March 5, 1977, p. 18.

"Nun's family and order arrange for baby's burial." *D&C*, May 2, 1976, p. B6.

"Nun's trial expected in November." D&C, September 1, 1976, p. B8

Bill Parker. "Nun's mental state part of defense," *D&C*, June 19, 1976, p. B1.

"Sister Maureen goes on trial Wednesday." *D&C*, February 12, 1977, p. B1.

John Stewart. "Aftermath: They're glad it's over." *D&C*, March 5, 1977, p. A1.

______. "April brought violent and bizarre crimes." *D&C*, May 4, 1976, p. B3.

________. "Newborn a Homicide: Found in Convent." *D&C*, April 29, 1976

________. "Brighton Nun Charged in Death of Infant." *D&C*, April 30, 1976, p. A1.

Maurice H. Thompson. "In church, a feeling of sadness." *D&C*, May 3, 1976, p. B1.

* * *

For *Mosquito Point Road:*

"Accepts Lawyer Court Assigned to Defend Her." *D&C*, April 9, 1920, p. 21.

"After Judge Delivers Charge This Morning Jury Will Get Odell Case." *D&C*, April 23, 1920, p. 37.

"Attorney May Ask Court to Permit Trial of Pearl Odell." *D&C*, April 25, 1920, p. 41.

"Conflicting Statements of Pearl Odell Are Offered By Prosecution." *D&C*, May 29, 1920, p. 21.

"Indictments in Kneip Case By Close of Week." *D&C*, January 14, 1920, p. 20.

"Both Defendant and His Wife Called to Stand in Murder Trial." *D&C*, April 22, 1920, p. 28.

"Confession Made By Pearl Odell To Be Read to Jury This Morning." *D&C*, May 28, 1920, p. 41.

"James Louis Odell Put to Death in Sing Sing Prison; Reported Calm Up to Last." *D&C*, April 29, 1921, p. 29.

"Jury, After Eleven Hours' Deliberation, Gives Verdict With Full Penalty of Law." *D&C*, April 24, 1920, p. 25.

"Jury For Trial of James L. Odell Completed in One Day; Wife To Go On Stand." D&C, April 20, 1920, p. 25.

"Mrs. Odell Will Decide Choice of Attorney To-day." D&C, April 7, 1920,

"Mrs. Odell's Father Visits Her in Jail." *D&C*, January 18, 1920, p. 36.

"Night Train Takes Odell to Sing Sing." *D&C*, April 27, 1920, p. 25.

"Odell and Wife Break Down As They Greet Each Other For First Time Since Trial." *D&C*, April 26, 1920, p. 25.

"Pearl Odell is Guilty in the Second Degree, Is Verdict After More Than Seven Hours of Deliberation." *D&C*, June 4, 1920, p. 33.

"Pearl Odell is Visited in Jail By Her Mother." *D&C*, January 16, 1920, p. 11.

"Pearl Odell Called to Witness Stand, Tells Story of Her Life." June 2, 1920.

"Pearl Odell Expected Jury to Acquit Her of Charge of Murdering Edward J. Kneip." *D&C*, June 5, 1920, p. 21.

"Pearl Odell to Testify This Afternoon In Behalf of Her Husband." *D&C*, April 21, 1920, p. 33.

"Public Danger in Free Use of Badge: Odell's Ruse Shows a Harm That One May Cause." *D&C*, January 15, 1920, p. 21.

"Taken in Taxicab to Lonely Spot, Young Man is Slain in Cold Blood: Murderer Named and Story of Killing Told in Two Statements to Authorities." *D&C*, January 9, 1920, p. 31.

"Trial of James L. Odell for Murder to Begin April 19th; His Wife's Trial Will Follow." D&C, April 1, 1920, p. 28.

"Will Take Up Murder Case Immediately." *D&C*, January 20, 1920, p. 1.

"Young Couple Accused of Brutal Murder Calm As They Face Charge in Court." *D&C*, January 10, 1920, p. 21.

* * *

For *Death of a First Baseman:*

"Another charged in murder." *Manhattan Mercury* (Manhattan, Kansas), April 6, 2005, p. 3.

Bowerman, Dan. "Former Chili resident slain in Kansas." *D&C*, March 2, 1982, p. 4B.

Brisendine, Steve. "Couple faced 10-20 years for murder." *Salina Journal*, May 13, 2006, p. A4.

"Cold Case Pinned on Soccer Mom." Abcnews.go.com, posted May 5, 2006, accessed March 17, 2020.

"Delaware woman found guilty of 23-year-old murder." *Marion Star* (Marion, Ohio), May 3, 2005, p. 2.

"Ex-Olathe woman faces trial in husband's death." *Manhattan Mercury*, July 2, 2004, p. 3.

Freile, Victoria E. "Dad waits 24 years to see son's killers sentenced." *D&C*, May 11, 2006, p. 1B.

Fuchs, Marek. *A Cold-Blooded Business*. New York: Skyhorse Publishing, 2014.

"Kansas murder case ends with plea." *D&C*, February 17, 2006, p. 2B.

"Killers were seeking bank keys." *The Iola Register*, March 2, 1982, p. 2.

Livadas, Greg. "Jury finds wife guilty of husband's 1982 murder." *D&C*, March 4, 2005, p. 13.

"Man convicted in 1982 fatal beating to be released Saturday." *Kmbc.com*, posted May 3, 2016, accessed March 25, 2020.

"Man enters guilty plea in 1982 killing." *Salina Journal* (Salina, Kansas), February 14, 2006, p. 3.

"Murder motive probed." *The Iola Register*, March 3, 1982, p. 6.

"Ohio woman charged in 1982 homicide fights extradition." *Fremont News-Messenger*, December 6, 2003, p. A5.

Pekarsky, Michelle and Shannon O'Brien "Johnson County woman walks out of prison after serving 9 years for husband's murder." *Fox4kc.com*, posted April 29, 2015, accessed March 25, 2020.

Rizzo, Tony. "Killer in infamous Olathe love triangle case soon will go free." *Kansascity.com*, posted May 2, 2016, accessed March 19, 2020.

______. "Parole nears for woman in 1982 Olathe love-triangle murder of David Harmon." *Kansascity.com*, posted April 25, 2015, accessed March 25, 2020.

"Suspects exist in banker's death." *St. Joseph News-Press*, March 4, 1982, p. 4B

"Woman charged in slaying back in Kansas." *Mansfield News-Journal*, January 10, 2004, p. 10A.

"Woman convicted of killing husband to testify against another defendant." *Dayton Daily News*, October 7, 2005, p. 13.

"Woman granted plea deal in husband's killing 24 years ago." *Marysville Journal-Tribune* (Marysville, Ohio), March 28, 2006, p. 5.

"Woman's arrest relieves Chili pair." *D&C*, December 10, 2003, p. 1B.

*　　*　　*

For *Pure/Evil:*

"Bach, Handel featured in musical arts concert." *The Item of Millburn and Short Hills,* June 10, 1982, p. 17.

"Beautiful music always starts with hard work." *The Central New Jersey Home News,* January 8, 1978, p. 59.

"City Man Faces 2 Rape Charges." *D&C,* November 15, 1973, p. 5B.

Craig, Gary. "Rapist confesses to 1991 murder." *D&C,* July 14, 2012, p. 1A.

"Family says the police have leads on missing daughter." *D&C,* August 7, 1991, p. 1B.

"Father of a missing Greece woman offers reward for information." *D&C,* December 24, 1991, p. 9A.

Galante, David. "Suspect charged in Barge Canal knifepoint robbery." *D&C,* February 14, 1984, p. 1B

Hernandez, Romel J. "Police perplexed by disappearance of ex-area woman." *The Central New Jersey Home News,* August 29, 1991, p. 1A.

Kava, Janine. "Autopsy: Teacher was slain." *D&C,* July 3, 1998, p. 3B.

_______. "Greece consults FBI on slayings." *D&C,* October 28, 1998, p. 2A.

Livadas, Greg. "Suspect in teacher's death already in jail." D&C, April 17, 1998, p. 1A.

______. "25-year history of violence marks suspect in death of Greece woman." D&C, April 17, 1998, p. 8A.

______, Amy Mayron, and Brian Kohn. "Remains found of missing teacher." *D&C,* April 16, 1998, p. 1A.

Kava, Janine. "Slain music teacher to be laid to rest." *D&C,* December 3, 1998, p. 3B.

McCombs, Mary. "Defense Team Presents New Theory in Brighton Ax Murder." *Spectrumlocalnews.com,* posted January 29, 2020, accessed March 30, 2020.

Mills, Steve. "Body raises fears of serial killer." *D&C,* October 13, 1992, p. 1A.

______ and Michael Wentzel. "Glare falls on area where bodies were found." *D&C,* October 30, 1992, p. 1A.

Morrell, Alan. "Patient accused of attacking guard." *D&C,* August 1, 2001, p. 2B.

"No leads yet on missing Greece woman." *D&C,* August 9, 1991, p. 2B.

Orr, Jim. "Vanished teacher leaves painful silence." *D&C,* August 16, 1991, 1A.

"Six Rabbits Rescued When Fire Hits Shed." *D&C,* May 7, 1967, p. 14B.

Wertheimer, Linda. "Skeleton is not yet identified." *D&C,* October 12, 1992, p. 9A.

"Woman's disappearance in August unexplained." *The Central New Jersey Home News*, December 17, 1991, p. 3.

"Yellow Barn will host composer George Crumb." *The Brattleboro Reformer* (Brattleboro, Vermont), July 25, 1982, p. 6.

Zeigler, Michael. "Sex abuser of teen is sentenced to 25 to life." *D&C*, June 28, 1994, p. 2B.

ACKNOWLEDGMENTS

Tekla Benson, Total Artistic Control; Max Dobson, Tech Director; Bob and Joyce Flesch; Pam Powell Friedler; Christine Green, photographer and writing buddy; Joan Lenhard, Director of Transportation; Mark Mariano, Jane Milliman, editor and publisher of *(585) Magazine*; Les McMahon; Robert Mladinich; Jim Munnings, Linda Powell; Donald A. Tubman, Boots on the Ground; R. Jerome Warren; Edwin and Sandy Yaw.

The trestle as it appears today, slowly sinking. (Photo by Christine Green)

AUTHOR'S NOTE

Although these are true stories, some names have changed to protect the privacy of the innocent. When possible, the spoken word has been quoted verbatim. However, when that is not possible, conversations have been reconstructed as closely as possible to reality based on the recollections of those who spoke and heard the words.

In places there has been a slight editing of spoken words, but only to improve readability. The denotations and connotations of the words remain unaltered. In some cases, witnesses are credited with verbal quotes that in reality only occurred in written form. Some characters may be composites.

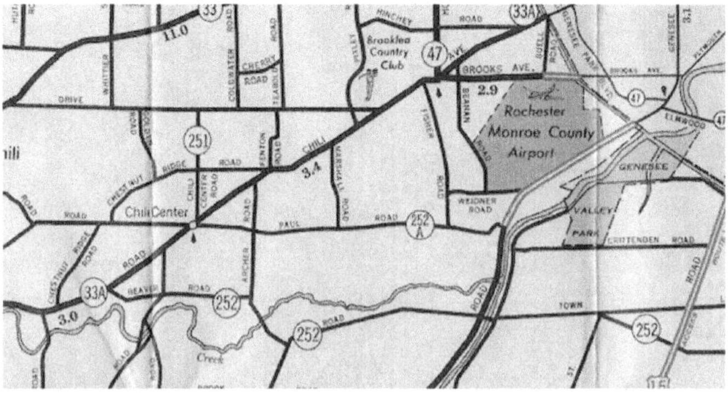

(Photo by Christine Green)

ABOUT THE AUTHOR

Michael Benson was born in Rochester and raised in Chili. Today, he is one of the world's most popular true-crime writers. His books—including *Nightmare in Rochester, Haunting Homicides* (both written with Private Investigator Donald A. Tubman), *Betrayal In Blood, Killer Twins* and *The Devil at Genesee Junction*—tell vividly of heinous criminals, their tragic victims, and the clever and stalwart lawmen who bring them to justice. On TV, he has twice been seen on ABC's *20/20* and is a regular commentator on the Investigation Discovery (I.D.), Oxygen, and HLN channels. He has appeared on *Murder in the Family with Geraldo Rivera, Inside Evil with Chris Cuomo, People Magazine Investigates, Deadly Sins, Southern Fried Homicide, The Killer You Thought You Knew, Evil Twins, Evil Stepmothers,* and *Evil Kin.*

During his four decades as a professional writer, Benson has worked closely with: a former gangster for biographies of Mafia dons Carmine Persico and Albert Anastasia, a retired Army Intelligence agent during the tense days after 9/11 for a book about the CIA, and a retired FBI agent for a book about National Security. He has co-written two books with a former New York Police Department "Cop of the Year"; explored the Grassy Knoll in Dallas with a former KGB agent while researching his highly-acclaimed *Who's Who in the JFK Assassination*; collaborated efficiently with an astronaut; and covered the Stephen Hayes triple-murder trial in New Haven, Ct., for the *New York Post*. Benson has a B.A. with honors in Communication Arts from Hofstra University. He is the winner of an Academy of American Poets award, and was in 2016 named a Wheatland-Chili High School Graduate of Excellence.

Made in the USA
Columbia, SC
05 June 2020

10214361R00134